Master Gemcutting Tips

A comprehensive collection of proven lapidary and gemcutting tips and methods that are of immediate and practical use to gemstone faceters, cabochon cutters, and carvers regardless of their experience.

By Gerald L. Wykoff, GG

Adamas Publishers
PO Box 5504
Washington, DC 20016
1-303-656-7050

® 1992 Gerald L. Wykoff GG

ALL RIGHTS RESERVED. PRINTED IN THE UNITED STATES OF AMERICA. NO PART OF THIS BOOK MAY BE REPRODUCED, STORED IN A RETRIEVAL SYSTEM OR TRANSMITTED, IN ANY FORM OR BY ANY MEANS, ELECTRONIC, MECHANICAL, OR BY PHOTO COPYING, RECORDING, OR OTHERWISE, WITHOUT THE PRIOR WRITTEN PERMISSION OF THE COPY-RIGHT HOLDER.

Library of Congress, Cataloging-in-Publication Data

Wykoff, Gerald L. 1930--
A comprehensive collection of lapidary and gemcutting tips and methods that are of immediate and practical use to gemstone faceters, cabochon cutters, and carvers regardless of their experience.
p.   cm.
Bibliogrphy p.
Includes index.
ISBN 0-9607892-7-8 : $17.95
TT212.W95 1992
739.1274--dc20

Contents

ABRASIVES
Make Diamond Paste..75
  Loose diamond powder is quite inexpensive and here is a way for you to make your own effective diamond paste of any grit size.

What Every Gemcutter Should Know About Abrasives..68
  To cut gemstones at the master level you should be familiar with the personality of most abrasives so here is a comprehensive listing and description of each.

ADHESIVES
Breaking the Superglue Bond.................................... 44
  A number of different techniques for breaking down superglue's adhesive attachment

Effective Method to Remove CA................................ 96
  Heat is a good approach for removing the bond made by a cyanoacrylate (superglue).

Use of Epoxy.. 56
  Epoxy use for dopping attracts a growing number of gemcutters because it's strong, versatile, clean—and can be made thicker.

Using Syringes For Fast Epoxy.................................. 89
  avoid messiness of two-part epoxies by using a pair of syringes.

CABOCHONS
Ridding a Buff of Contamination..............................143
  A chunk of contaminant on a polishing buff can drive a gemcutter dizzy and here is an effective counter, a way to rid your buff of hard trouble-making particles.

Making Interesting Cabochons....................................2
  Utilizing press-on graphics letters to produce innovative cabochon shapes.

Special Techniques For Cabochons............................ 45
  Various master techniques for cabochon cutting, including use of analysis of slope and apex positioning with the Barnett Gauge.

Cutting Grooves and Channels.................................. 58
  Those fancy grooves and channels you see on the Munsteiner

(Fantasy) cuts are easy to perform on a dressed silicon carbide wheel.

DESIGNS

Bill Horton's "Drunken Oval".................................. 119
    The easy-to-follow design steps used by a Supreme Master Gemcutter to produce a unique cabochon shape.

For Brilliance Cut a Sunflower............................. 115
    Here are plan views and cutting instructions for the new series of colored diamond cutting designs developed by De Beers—and which are suitable for colored stone faceting.

DOPPING

A Dopping Technique.. 8
    A way to use wooden dowels and nails as dopsticks with hints on removing the stones when you're finished.

Different Approaches to Dopping........................ 145
    Regardless of the type of gemcutting you do, here are a number of approaches and adhesives used in dopping that you should be familiar with.

Dopping Method Relies on Shellac...................... 18
    A fast dopping method which relies on shellac.

DRILLING

Drilling Small Holes in Gemstones...................... 93
    Invariably a gemcutter will be faced with the need to drill a small hole in a gemstone: here's an inexpensive way.

FACETING

Tips on Faceting... 3
    Painting facets, avoiding the nuisance of screws and hex wrenches, and removing the danger of striking the arbor nut.

A Way to Cut Even Break Facets............................ 4
    By coning a pavilion first, break facets can be cut quickly and evenly, with less chance of error.

For Good Results Use Tangents............................ 14
    A hand calculator is useful for figuring out how to change

the angles on a facet design.

Faceting With "Ticks"... 79
"listen and look" is also a good rule for faceters to follow
and the "tick" is the thing to listen for.

Cut Table First, Then Relax and Cut........................ 91
An optional sequence for faceting, cutting the table first,
is presented here.

GEMOLOGY

Some Comments on Serpentine................................ 18
There's much more to Serpentine than just spelling it.

Heat Treating... 22
Yogo Gulch sapphires are among the world's prettiest—but
often only after heat treatment.

Suggestions For Best Universal Faceting Angles......... 37
Recent raytrace studies show that an acceptable set of angles
suitable for all gemstones does indeed exist.

Interpreting Imperfections...................................... 99
Understanding what is going on when certain visual conditions
reveal themselves on a gem material being cut.

Troy vs. Avoirdupois... 138
Getting a good mental grip on weights and measures in
lapidary work isn't easy but here is a complete list of the
most important standards.

GRINDING

Technique For Scratch Identification........................ 16
You should be able to interpret the various scratches that
you'll encounter during grinding and polishing operations.

"Running the Wheel" is Important Cab Technique...... 82
Most cabbers don't cut a cabochon properly because they fail to use
the abrasive wheel properly: here's how to do it right.

LAPS

Cleaning Pelletized Resin Laps................................. 22
You can easily and thoroughly clean a pelletized resin lap

v

by using a 3M scouring pad and some soap and water.

Resurfacing Laps..25
   Lap surfaces become disfigured after extensive use and here
   is a procedure for resurfacing them yourself.

Lap Tips From Experts...63
   You may or may not have a wide variety of laps and wheels but
   regardless, disciplined use of your cutting tools will produce
   superior gemstones.

Thin Polishing Laps Gain Acceptance......................105
   More and more gemcutters are opting for thin plastic
   impregnated polishing laps because of cost, ease of use, and
   repeatability problems...here is a complete description
   of most of the new polishing lap technology.

Laps: Cast Iron Laps are Useful...1
   Why cast iron laps are useful for grinding and polishing, and
   how to correct certain defects in the lap manufacture.

Making Your Own Laps..66
   Regardless of the type gemcutting you do, laps can be expensive so
   here is a technique for making your own diamond laps.

Cliff Jackson's Wax Lap... 102
   Follow this procedure for easily making wax laps for polishing
   (even flat lapping) on softer stones.

MARKETING

Which Shape Sells Best..6
   A survey among gemcutters gives some indication into which
   shapes people prefer.

The 7 Points of Payoff Profits.......................................13
   Here are seven tips on realizing greater profits from your
   gemcutting activities.

POLISH

Consistent Polish Requires a System......................... 121
   You have to have a disciplined system in your approach to gem
   polishing is you expect to get maximum results.

Oxalic Acid Polish..9
   Oxalic acid on leather imparts a marvelous polish on silicate
   minerals.

Techniques on Ceramic Polishing..............................12
   A proven procedure for obtaining good polishing results with
   a ceramic polishing lap.
Channel Polisher? Try a Toothbrush......................20
   An old electric toothbrush is an excellent tool for polishing
   channels and other intricate areas.
Polishing Buffs and Polishes..................................21
   A listing of the various materials used for polishing and the
   polishes that are regarded as their best supplement.
Ceramic Laps...24
   An optional technique for getting the most out of ceramic
   polishing laps.
Solving Difficult Polishing Problems.....................25
   The PH factor is extremely important when it comes to solving
   the reluctance of some gem materials to come up to polish.
Colloidal Silica Proves Very Effective Gemstone Polish..31
   A new chemical polish, colloidal silica, is highly effective
   but it does have some severe drawbacks.
Use Baby Shampoo With Diamond...........................92
   Here is the quickest, easiest, most effective way to make your
   own diamond paste.

REPAIRS
Tips on Repair Work..9
   A 24-karat flash plate on a gold jewelry item after repair
   work makes it glisten like new, to the customer's delight.
Special Dopstick For Ring Repairs........................93
   A special dopstick that will hold a ring in place firmly so
   you can facet or cab on the stone without removal problems.
Cutter Prepares Release Form................................95
   When you do repair work which might not be expensive you still
   face a liability problem for the cost of a stone or the entire
   jewelry piece, so here's a sample release form that you might
   want your customers to sign before you accept the work.

SAWING
A Sawing Technique..7
   Lining a saw's jaws with rubber provides solid grip on stone.

Carving Techniques With a Saw.................................... 33
    Don't overlook the benefits that a diamond saw can provide when you are carving or involved in bulk removal.

Quick Sawing.. 55
    Procedures for quickly removing bulk from crystals using the lapidary saw.

STONES
Paua Shells Beautiful—But Dangerous......................35
    Use caution when cutting paua shells because the swarf and debris is toxic.

Techniques For Cutting Sunstones............................27
    Sunstones pose an orientation and a cutting challenge and here is the procedure for coming up with an excellent cut each time.

Tips in Corundum Polishing....................................... 80
    Corundum when properly polished shows a marvelous subadamantine luster and the good polishing techniques given here will produce such results.

Star Sapphire Height is Optional................................99
    Don't be misled into thinking that a star sapphire is a failure unless it contain a high apex.

Opal Cutting/Polishing... 125
    Opal represents one of the greatest—and most exciting— challenges in gemcutting: here are generally accepted approaches for good results with this remarkable gemstone material.

TECHNIQUE
Marking Girdles.. 97
    Here is an easy way to polish girdles on a faceted stone, but the technique is also useful for cabs.

Avoiding a Shower When Girdling............................ 98
    You and your equipment can get wet when the splash pan gate is open for girdling so use a wick and a paper clip to control the splash.

A Trick For Even Girdles.. 122
    If you don't have a pre-forming tool, a length of waxed string can provide you with a setup that produces even girdles.

Proper Lighting is Important...120
  To monitor the progress of your gemcutting you should have
  proper lighting that is properly arranged to produce the best
  view.

Papier-Maché For Unique Jewelry................................123
  The nice thing about that old standby, papier-maché, is that
  it's easy to use, to paint, and to produce a quick, interesting piece of
  jewelry that will accommodate nearly any gem shape.

Do You Really Need Angle Splitters..........................141
  An angle splitter is admittedly a nice supplemental tool on
  a faceting machine but careful technique will produce the
  same, precise results.

WORKSHOP

Good Holder For Printing..11
  3-hole punched Acetate holders are excellent for protecting
  drawings and instructions near your work station.

Saving Contents..21
  It's difficult to open a can of liquid material and then re-
  seal it without the possibility that the contents will be
  ruined: here's a good tip to avoid this problem.

Construction of a 1/10 Vernier...................................65
  For faceters who want to split angles on their faceting
  machine, a vernier isn't a must, but here's how to make one
  for the sake of convenience.

Good Use For Ceramic Laps...76
  Don't throw that old, ineffective ceramic lap away because it has a
  new life as a master lap in polishing.

How to Make a Polariscope..104
  A polariscope is probably the one gemological instrument that
  every gemcutter—especially faceters—should possess and know
  how to use...and here's how to make an inexpensive one.

Removing Oil..3
  An oil absorbing chemical used by machinists can remove oil
  from your lapidary workshop.

The Big Fight Against Rust..6
  A squirt of WD 40 goes a long ways in eliminating rust, plus a
  unique dopstick for use in repair work.

PREFACE

It's no great secret that many gemcutters are self taught.

Even for such a commendable approach to the excitement in gemcutting, it does pose great difficulties for individuals.

The most serious shortcoming of the self teaching route rests in the difficulty of bringing all the elements of gemcutting into a discipline whole. So many nuances and technicalities of the craft take years to learn through the aged technique of trial and error. If the error does not occur or the conditions fail to develop in just the proper sequence or orientation a valuable lesson is lost.

Learning lapidary is difficult enough without the additional—and unnecessary—penalty of re-inventing the craft. That's why this book, *Master Gemcutting Tips*, was written. It is intended to unveil tips, techniques, methods, and procedures used or originated by master gemcutters who are willing to share their expertise with others.

The subjects in this book came either from members of the American Society of Gemcutters or from my own teaching and writing experiences. They've all been proven.

If only one of the many ideas presented here is of value to a gemcutter and will allow him or her to proceed with the lapidary craft in an easier, more enjoyable, or more effective way then the book's purpose is fulfilled. And if the suggestions here allow the gemcutter to produce finer and more beautiful gems, then truly the sharing of ideas is totally justified.

Gerald L. Wykoff, CMG GG

Master Gemcutting Tips

Cast Iron Laps are Useful . . .

Most gemcutters will agree that when it comes to polishing, a cast iron lap plate is infinitely superior to a steel lap. What provides the advantage is the porosity of the iron lap. Yet many lapidary artists mistakenly shy away from a cast iron lap just because of this alleged defect.

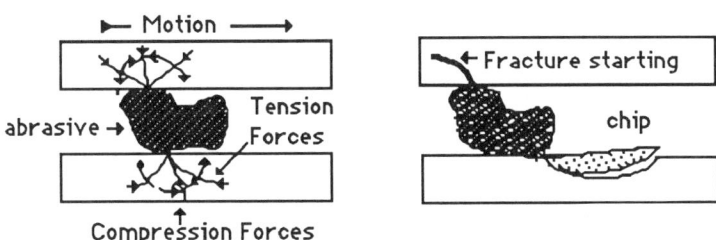

Grit doesn't roll on a cast iron lap as much as it does on a steel or ceramic lap. The small surface flaws such as sand holes or gas holes provide a reservoir for diamond particles to drop into. Consequently, the particles remain "pocketed" where their edges are exposed to work on a crystal that is brought against the lap. This same explanation describes the difference between porous ceramic laps (which are made Graves especially for lapidary) and ordinary ceramic computer discs. The specially formulated ceramic laps offer a pocket for diamond particles whereas a hard, flat surface forces the grit to roll and thus cause scratches.

In some cases, though, the holes in a cast iron lap are too large. As a result, diamond and cutting swarf eventually build up to form an unwanted bump. The way to handle this condition is to drill a tiny hole all the way through the lap so

Master Gemcutting Tips

grit may fall through into the pan. You can use a tiny wire to punch through the hole to keep it open.

Making Interesting Cabochons . . .

Paul Melford of Cleveland, OH, is forever searching out new ways to create and cut interesting—and marketable—cabochons.

He has now taken to the arts and graphics store to purchase large press-on letter templates. From these, Paul presses a letter on a slab of mineral and then carefully cuts out the letters with a slab saw and a hand diamond wire saw. He uses a diamond drill to make cutouts for such letters as "R," "O," "P","A," "D," etc. He then finishes each letter in traditional cab style.

The backs of the letters are carefully flat lapped to assure that each letter is the same thickness. Once the letters are finished, Paul flat laps a thin mineral background slab piece and glues the letters onto this. Depending on how the customer intends to use and display the work, Paul glues a

Master Gemcutting Tips

hook to the rear, sets up an easel prop or even attaches the stone piece to a frame covered with green felt. In some cases, the backpieces have been made with glass or mirror. With a mirror, the reflected view of the thick letters lends a spectacular optical effect. When a colored background is desired, a sheet of colored acetate is attached to the bottom of a glass backpiece and the stones are glued on the top. Paul uses a clear 5-Minute Epoxy, moving each letter in a circular manner over the epoxy until all of the bubbles have been removed. The results can be spectacular.

Removing Oil . . .

Getting oil off a stone that's just been sawed or worked can be a messy affair.

It isn't messy, though, if you fill a box with such special oil absorbing compounds as "Hi-Dri" (or a similar product) . Service stations use this material to keep oil off the floors. Just take an oil smeared slab and drop it into the sawdust-like substance and in no time at all, the oil be absorbed off the surface.

Various Tips on Faceting . . .

Jim Pilsner of St. Louis, MO, says when faceting he paints all pre-polished facets with an insoluble ink and then proceeds to polish off the ink. It only takes a few moments to paint a stone's surface. As the ink comes off the polish goes on and you are always assured of a good visual inspection to assure yourself of a comprehensive polish on each facet.

Also, to avoid all the nuisance of tiny set screws and hex

Master Gemcutting Tips

Don't overlook the benefit of a nonsoluble ink pen for painting facets. In polishing, you remove the ink and evaluate your progress. Ink also marks girdle facets nicely so you can keep facets stacked over each other.

wrenches, remove the quill's set screw (if that is how it locks!) that confirms the grip on dopsticks and replace it with a small wingnut. This way you can tighten or loosen the dopsticks easily and conveniently. The only time the wingnut gets in the way is when you want to girdle—and even then you can sometimes avoid having to take out the wingnut.

Another faceting suggestion: always put tape around an exposed arbor nut—or at least stretch a heavy, thick rubber band around its outer perimeter. This protects against any stone damage in case you absent-mindedly run the stone against the lock down nut.

A Way to Cut Even Break Facets . . .

On rounds, especially round brilliants, go into free-wheeling and first cone your pavilion at 42 degrees. Then cut your girdle breaks at 43 degree so their bottom tips meet to form an equal ring around the culet. This pro-

Master Gemcutting Tips

vides assurance that the girdle shape is perfectly round. Now cut the mains at 42 degrees. Using this kind of method not only allows you to cut the breaks to the same depth, but you can do it with little error.

Here's how to hook up a light facet depth sensor for the Graves faceting machine. [*This idea has been published before but it works this way:*]

Get a Light Emitting Diode (LED) with a 10,000 ohm resistor and a small 1.5v battery. Hook each lead into the matching stop blocks on the quill. As the quill drops down from cutting the two energized stop block surfaces approach each other. When they're close, the LED flickers. Of course, when they touch the light comes on steady, indicating that the facet is finished at the desired height.

Incidentally, for those of you who have a metal splash pan try splitting a section of vinyl—or rubber—hose and fitting it around the rim of the splash pan. That way when you lose a stone you'll have a soft cushion for it to hit up

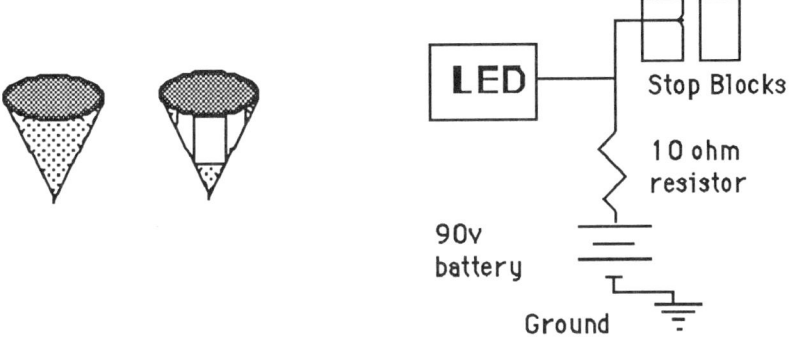

It's extra work to cone a pavilion first, but that way you can lay in facets with more accuracy. On the right is a diagram for making a facet detector with

Master Gemcutting Tips

against—before it drops down onto the bottom of the pan.

Which Shape Sells Best?

If you're looking at a piece of mineral or crystal and wondering what shape you should cut for the market, here are the results of a gemcutter survey.

A public balloting was held in 1992 to determine what shapes of faceted gems were most preferred. This was conducted at the biannual rock and gem show of the Neville Public Museum Geology Club of Green Bay, WI.

The display gems were all cut from clear 24% lead glass to the same approximate size and were in a Riker mount. The people in attendance were encouraged to vote by the promise than an amethyst in the shape of their choice would be cut for them if their names were drawn. The popularity results were as follows:

1. Emerald......................16.1%
2. Navette........................15.2%
3. Pendaloque..................15.1
4. Pentagon.....................10.8
5. Oval............................10.0
6. Octagon.......................7.5
7. Hexagon......................7.2
8. Round..........................6.6
9. Triangle......................6.5
10. Square.........................1.56

The Big Fight Against Rust . . .

Guy Fender of Olympia, WA, fights the big battle against rust the same as other lapidaries.

Master Gemcutting Tips

To Guy, rust is "...the bugaboo in using water with all diamond cutting tools. I just run my laps, etc. until they are dry then give them a squirt of WD 40 and wipe them off.

"I am now testing auto radiator rust preventative—using it as directed for an auto radiator.

"A gemcutter can always use water soluble oil that is available at any machine shop. It's simply mixed with water and used when grinding."

Guy also came up with his own version of a good repair dopstick, stating that he has been using his own version that he made some time ago. Below is an illustration of Guy's special dopstick.

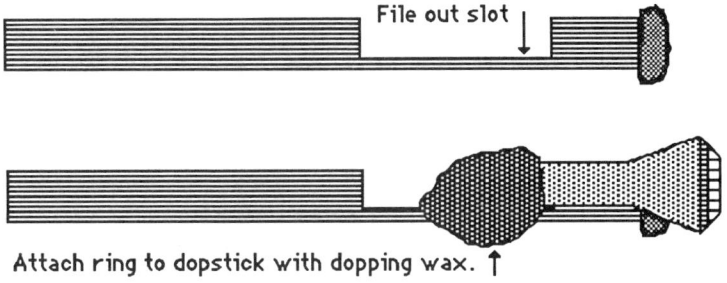

Attach ring to dopstick with dopping wax. ↑

He uses a long slot in the dopstick to accommodate different ring sizes and locks the ring onto the dopstick with a large gob of dop wax. With the ring locked on, Guy sets the dopstick in a 45° adaptor and works directly on the stone, mostly by adjusting the elevation of the quill head.

Saw Technique...

Having trouble holding an irregular piece of mineral in the vice for sawing? Or you're afraid that pressure on

Master Gemcutting Tips

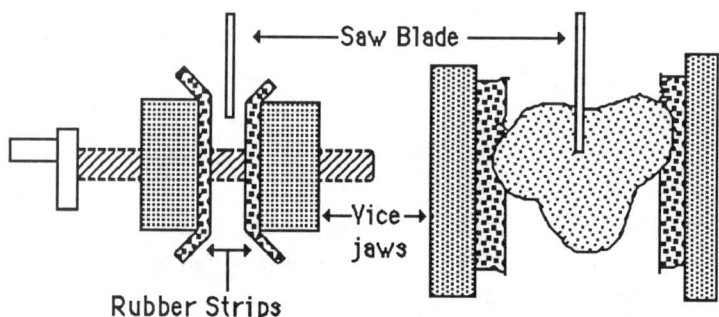

the vice jaws will damage the stone?

Try lining the jaws of the vice with a section cut out of a automobile tire or inner tube. The rubber grips very tightly under pressure yet keeps the stone from damage or moving.

A Dopping Technique...

If you use 5-Minute Epoxy and wooden dowels for dopsticks on your cabs, there's a convenient way to remove the stone.

Just saw the stone off close to the attachment. Then use a hot knife to cut the cured epoxy away.

You can use a variation of this method by employing nails as dopsticks. The benefit of a nail is that you can apply heat to the end of the nail with a torch and the heat will transfer up to the epoxy where it will destroy the bond.

And remember, 5-Minute Epoxy is just that. You

Master Gemcutting Tips

can put considerable strain on an attachment within 8-10 minutes after setting up the bond; it isn't necessary to wait for an hour or so. To keep the Epoxy from becoming too messy to work with, pour in a little cornstarch when you mix the two parts. It works wonders as a thickener.

Oxalic Acid Polish...

For gemcutters wanting an extra fine polish on quartz or onyx, here's a tip from Mexican artisans.

There is a shortage of lapidary power tools in Mexico so quartz-onyx workers there use oxalic acid on leather. This ruins the leather in short order but it does impart a fine finish on the minerals' surface.

If you wish to avoid acid (and sometimes its attendant fumes), stick to cerium oxide on leather. It also gives a good polish—although a touch of oxalic acid in addition to the cerium will do wonders to the polish.

Tips on Repair Work . . .

Many gemcutters perform repair work for jewelers

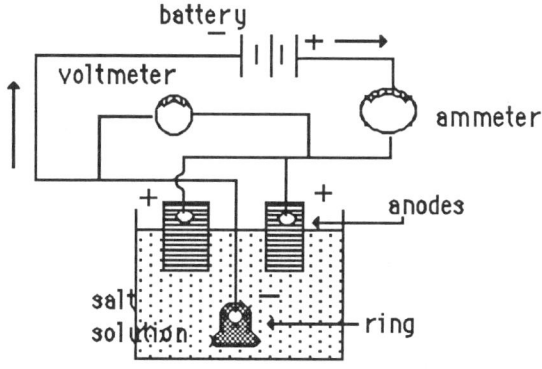

Master Gemcutting Tips

and this (as much as possible) involves working on a stone that remains in the mounting.

It's good business practice to return an attractive jewelry item when finished and this would, of course, involve cleaning up the mounting a bit. What's a good way to address this without going into a complete goldsmith shop?

Answer: You can set up completely for about $10. Go buy yourself a 6-or 9-volt dry cell battery, a couple lengths of thin copper wire (say, about 12 inches long) a glass bowl, and a 2" x .5" strip of stainless steel.

Also, buy yourself a small amount of Electro-Cleaner from any lapidary supply store. That will set you up with a electrolysis unit which just about every goldsmith shop has.

If you want to clean up gold or silver jewelry, just hook the jewelry piece up to the positive anode of the battery and the stainless steel strip to the negative cathode. Place the two items in the electro-cleaner bath and watch the bubbles fly. It'll take about 10 seconds to give the jewelry item a thorough cleaning.

Here's a cute trick that many goldsmiths use and it fascinates customers. Give the jewelry mounting a flash plate after you've electro cleaned it. For this you'll need another stainless steel strip and another bowl to hold the gold plating solution and you can buy non-cyanide solution (from Delmar, Mfg of Chicago).

Plating is opposite to cleaning. Just connect the mounting to the negative cathode and the stainless steel to the positive anode. Now the electrical current will carry the gold particles in the solution to the negative cathode eg., the jewelry metal, and deposit it there. Presto! In 10-15 seconds you'll have a piece of jewelry that looks like it

Master Gemcutting Tips

just came off a set of polishing wheels.

Good Holder For Printing . . .

Maintaining printed design instructions in good condition and free of splashes is a task that most gemcutters have faced at one time or another.

A number of gemcutters have added a nice touch by purchasing plastic sheet protectors—the kind you'll find in any office supply store— for each of their designs.

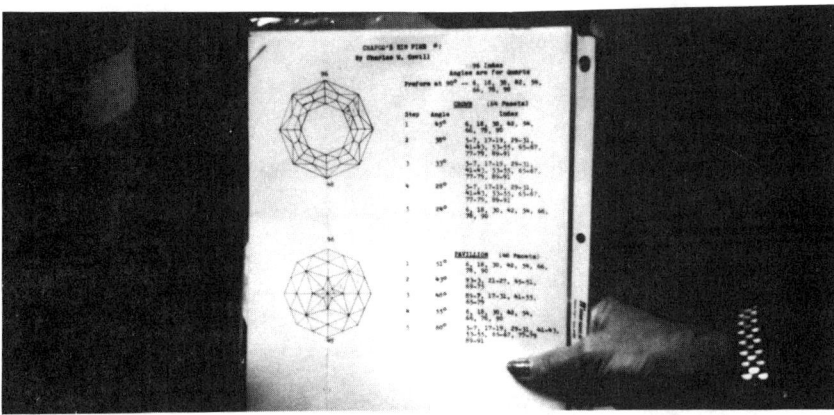

Each design is placed in the sheet protector and then inserted in a 3-ring binder (the protectors are 3-hole punched). This way, you can take the design out, hang it or hold it close to your faceting machine—and even write on the plastic cover with a felt tipped pen when necessary. The plastic covering is also handy for water protection.

The writing comes right off with a Kleenex or towel and a bit of alcohol.

A box of 100 protectors are sold by many office supply stores and catalogers for about $15.00.

Master Gemcutting Tips

Techniques on Ceramic Polishing . . .

Getting a ceramic polishing lap to polish is a major challenge for many faceters. Too often they just can't seem to get acceptable results.

That's not the problem for James Gray of Asheville, NC. Here's a method—used by many faceters—that this national Pinnacle Award winning faceter uses:

1. run the ceramic lap at medium speed while pressing to it a paper towel containing lacquer thinner.

2. shake a diamond spray well, and spray four (4) one-second shots on the turning ceramic lap for a base coat.

3. with a paper towel, wipe all the diamond spray you can off the slow running lap.

4. spray one two-second shot on the lap and wipe very lightly.

Master Gemcutting Tips

The lap is now ready for polishing (make certain you use a lapidary ceramic lap: it's the only one that contains the highly desirable porous surface where diamond particles can reside). There will develop a creamy substance around the facet being polished. When this creamy substance begins to reduce (nearly disappear) around the facet, it is time to move to another area of the lap or recharge.

To recharge repeat steps 3 and 4. After recharging three times, repeat steps 1-2-3-4. To polish a large table start at the beginning with steps 1-2-3-4.

Before transferring and when the stone is finished wipe the polished areas with lacquer thinner and wash the lap thoroughly with dish detergent.

Note: Some faceters don't wash the lap after use. They place it in a dedicated plastic bag for storage until the next time.

The 7 Points of Payoff Profits . . .

It takes discipline and a procedure to produce profits in lapidary. Here is the 7-step procedure formula by Texas' Herb Hirata for making his gemcutting skills pay off:

1. prevent early burnout of expensive laps by careful attention and maintenance eg., don't engage in heavy material removal with fine laps.

2. proper lighting—use good, well directed lighting so you can evaluate your work properly.

3. simple dopping—use the KISS method (Keep It Strictly Simple).

4. polish—increase lap speed slightly when using diamond polish.

Master Gemcutting Tips

5. Experience—The more stones you cut, the better mastery of different patterns and techniques you will have. Rely upon the "Banker's Rule" ie., you can't make any withdrawals if you haven't already made deposits. Experience and experimenting are great deposits.

6. Sources for Rough and Equipment—Keep everlastingly at it: keep looking for new, better suppliers.

7. Wholesale Buying—Get yourself a state tax number (it's cheap and easy) so you can get into the wholesale buyer sections at shows and exhibits.

For Good Results Use Tangents . . .

Have you ever used the Tangent Ratio formula in changing the angles on a facet design?

It's a formula worth knowing and practicing. Why? When you merely add to or subtract from given angles you change the plan design of the cut and this often causes difficulties. In other words, the design doesn't really work out the way it was supposed to.

By using the Tangent Ratio you change the angles according to the critical angle of a new crystal variety but keep the integrity of the plan view.

Here's an easy hand calculator way worked out by Elton McCawley and reported by Martin Bliefernich of Newburg, OR. The following units are buttons that will need to be pressed on the hand calculator.

TAN
M+
MR
=
X

Master Gemcutting Tips

SHIFT or INVERT
./. (division sign)

Here's a sample problem. You have a design in which the angles for diamond/CZ are given. You want to facet the design with angles for quartz. The pavilion main angle for diamond/CZ = 40.6 degrees. The pavilion main angle for quartz = 43.2

If the angles for the CROWN mains are available, the process works just as well.

Here is the procedure:
1. Enter the Quartz angle (43.2)
2. Press **TAN** (.9391)
3. Press ./.
4. Enter CZ angle (40.6)
5. Press **TAN** (.8571)
6. Press = (1.0956) This number will remain in Memory Recall (after Step 7) unless you negate it. This factor is necessary for further calculations beginning with Step 8.
7. Press **M+** (1.0956 goes into memory)
8. Enter any known CZ angle eg., pavilion break = 41.7

Master Gemcutting Tips

9. Press **TAN** (.89097)
10. Press **X**
11. Press **MR** (1.0956)
12. Press = (.97616)
13. Press **SHIFT** or **INVERT**
14. Press **TAN** (44.3) The resulting number (44.3 degrees) is the corresponding pavilion break angle for quartz.

You can use this formula to work out all angles.

Technique For Scratch Ident . . .

Can you recognize the different scratches and conditions on the surface of a facet or polished cab?

As your experience grows in gemcutting, it's vital that you're able to interpret the various scratch conditions. That way you'll be able to respond immediately to correct the lap condition.

Here is a rundown on various scratches from the book *Master Faceting* by Gerald Wykoff.

The culprit is often aggregation and flow, but not alwways. Surface defects show up abruptly, unexpectedly—and challenge you to find the answer.

Smoothing Lap Marks—these marks stand out against the velvet-like pre-polish finish and often reflect little more than inadequate pre-polishing (sometimes the result of contamination of a prepolishing lap). They can usually be removed by further pre-polishing—but definitely should be removed prior to polishing.

Deep Scratches Running Partially Across Facet—it takes a fraction of time for polishing grains to ball up under a facet and then begin scratching. That's why polish-

Master Gemcutting Tips

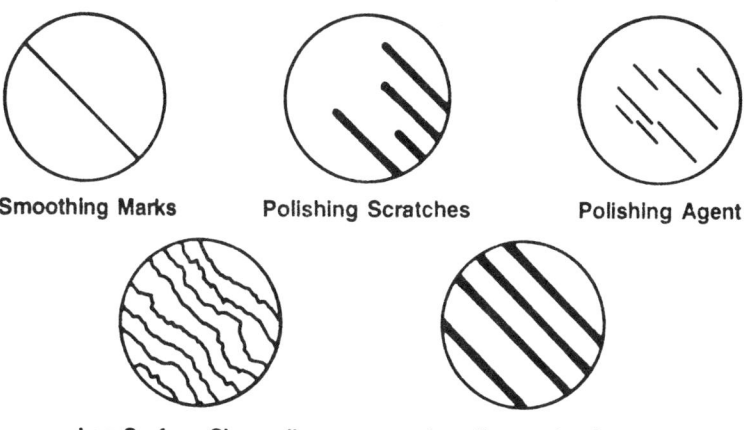

ing scratches attributed to aggregation and flow usually slice into the trailing half of the facet. Check the lap: it probably needs scoring or cleaning.

Thin, Light Scratches Not Completely Across Facet— when scratches like this suddenly show up, it's often a problem with the polishing agent. It's probably been applied too thick, dried out, and/or is not covering different areas of the lap. Try adding some lubricant or thinning the polishing mix. **Remember**: oxide polishes should be applied in a thin, wet-dry, slurry manner.

Uneven Facet Surface or Channeling—tiny ruts on a polished facet are often caused by polishing the facet in a stationary position so that lap surface irregularities are transferred to the facet. Sweep the facet across the lap a few times with moderate pressure and you'll minimize this condition.

Parallel Scratches Completely Across a Facet-— almost always you'll be dealing with contamination when a scratch runs from one edge of a facet to the other. Clean

Master Gemcutting Tips

the lap thoroughly or search for the contaminant and remove it. If the problem is with the polish, discard it. Check the stone, too, to make certain a crumbled edge or open flaw isn't feeding tiny chips to the wheel.

Dopping Method Relies on Shellac . . .

Richard C. McAllister of Palm Bay, FL, who teaches faceting at the Southeast Federation Wildacres workshop, follows an effective procedure for dopping.

Here is Richard's method:
1. Grind a false table
2. Dop stone to flat dopstick using superglue
3. Cut and polish pavilion (and girdle)
4. Transfer using Stick Shellac.

While using the Facetron type jig, lock both dopsticks in position after melting shellac and push the stone into the cone or "V" dopstick, heat the dopstick that has the superglue, destroying the CA bond. Then allow the dopsticks to cool to room temperature. Usually at this point, when the dopsticks are unlocked, the superglued dopstick drops off with very little effort.

5. Removing the finished stone is very simple. Just refrigerate and the stone pops off. Clean up is very simple. A little Acetone.

Bingo!

Some Comments on Serpentine . . .

A gemcutter sent away to a mail order rough supplier, asking for a nice green serpentine that he could cab. Later, he received a package from the dealer who sent him a stone that was identified as, "Pelhamine."

Master Gemcutting Tips

Did the gemcutter get what he ordered?

What he got from the dealer is exactly what he'd ordered. Pelhamine is a variety of grayish-green serpentine from Pelham, MA, and it usually takes a superior polish.

Keep in mind that serpentine is divided into three major divisions—Antigorite, Chrysotile, and Lizardite. There are many varieties of serpentine. Many of their names have little present day usage.

Here are some of the better known ones:

Common

Bastite—enstatite altered more or less completely to serpentine.

Bowenite—a hard compact form of antigorite.

Metataxite—type of serpentine from Silesia (Poland).

Pelhamine—a grayish-green serpentine, capable of a fine polish, found near Pelham, MA.

Precious or Noble

Serpentine—the name applied to the translucent serpentines used for ornamentation.

Picrolite—a type of antigorite serpentine.

Polyphant stone—a serpentinous diabase from Cornwall, England.

Pseudophite (Styrian "jade")—an aluminous serpentine found in Styria and elsewhere in Austria.

Retinalite—a massive yellow to light oil green serpentine with a waxy lustre.

Ricolite—a fine-grained serpentine with colored bands from Rico, NM.

Satelite—a fibrous serpentine found in CA and MD. Cut as a cat's eye.

Schiller spar—optional name for Bastite.

Master Gemcutting Tips

Serpentinite—name applied to the rock-like types of serpentine.

Thermophyllite—variety name for a serpentine from Finland.

Williamsite—attractive noble serpentine found in TX.

Zermattite—type of serpentine from Zermatt, Switzerland.

Channel Polisher? Try a Toothbrush . . .

Looking for an instrument to polish out channels, grooves and other difficult-to-get-at cuts?

Try an old electric toothbrush. It posseses a rapid reciprocating action and a wedged shape piece of felt superglued to the plastic holder works like dynamite.

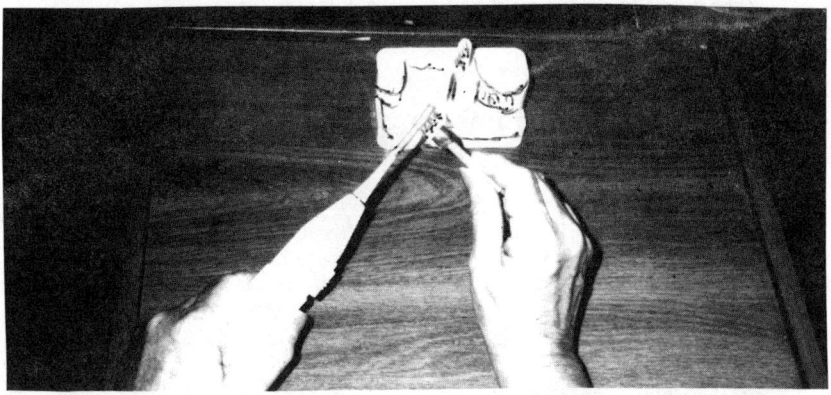

Gemcutters who've used an electric toothbrush polisher claim that the toothbrush is also great for polishing gold and silver. Look for one at the local flea market or in a yard sale. Replace the bristles with a felt or leather pad (the bristles will work but they consume considerable time).

Master Gemcutting Tips

Polishing Buffs and Polishes . . .

Here is a listing of the most common polishing buffs and laps and the compounds generally used with each:

Canvas...with tin oxide.

Felt...with cerium oxide, tin oxide, chrome oxide or Linde A.

Leather...with chrome oxide, Linde A, tin oxide, rouge, diamond paste.

Lucite...with tin oxide, cerium oxide or Linde A. Ultra Laps are also used extensively on Lucite laps.

Maple...with diamond paste, tripoli, Linde A or tin oxide

. *Pellon*...with colloidal silica, tin oxide, Linde A, or chrome oxide.

Tin...with Linde A.

Velour...with tin oxide or alumina oxide, Linde A.

Saving the Contents...

Here is an old carpenter's trick for saving the contents of materials that harden in a can:

If you open a can of paint, resin, varnish, wood stain or similar material that tends to harden and become unusable after resealing just fill up the can with clean, smooth stones so the liquid comes clear to the top.

This squeezes out the air—which promotes thickening—and the material will remain liquid for months afterwards. Use a quartz, flint, chert, or chalcedony as filler. Don't use hematite (the liquid will be the color of blood when you re-open the can) or gypsum (it'll dissolve).

Master Gemcutting Tips

Cleaning Pelletized Resin Laps...

To clean pelletized resin laps such as Crystalite's Last Lap and get them working beautifully again, take a page from the tips offered by C. A. Colbraugh, of Kingman, AZ. Cut a 3M stripping pad, either the black or green—into 2.5 inch pads. With a good stream of water, hold the pads on the Last Laps with considerable pressure at moderate polishing speed.

Colbraugh even spreads a couple of tablespoons of wheat on the lap before commencing with the cleaning. He claims the green pad will give a finer finish thanks to the wheat.

Heat Treating...

Yogo Gulch sapphires can be among the prettiest of gemstones—but they often need a bit of heat treatment. Here are a couple techniques:

Roll out a couple of 1/2 inch thick clay patties and

Master Gemcutting Tips

place the sapphires between, sandwich style. Make sure none of the stones touch each other. Place in a kiln and heat at 2,000° F for four hours. The trick is to increase heat 100° every 10 minutes until you reach the 2000° F.

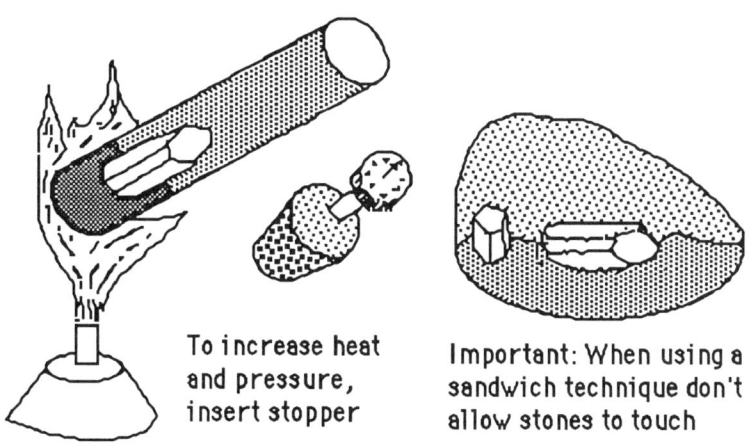

To increase heat and pressure, insert stopper

Important: When using a sandwich technique don't allow stones to touch

level. Remain at that temperature for at least 4 hours.
Or,
Place the sapphire in a 6"-8" long test tube which is about 1-1.5 in. diameter. Fill the tube with white and black (titanium) sand (tamp the sand well) as shown in the illustration.

Allow the stone to remain slightly on top of the sand so you can monitor the color change. Plug the end and insert a pyrometer to measure temperature.

Heat the test tube on a Bunsen burner at 1400 degrees F for 2-6 hours—or until you achieve the color change you want. Lower the heat slowly.

Master Gemcutting Tips

Ceramic Laps...

Loren A. Taylor, of Alameda, CA, offers a few tips on benefits obtained by polishing with a Ceramic lap.

Loren had been having no luck with polishing gems until trying out the ceramic lap—and then matters improved immeasurably. Now the California gemcutter uses only the ceramic lap for polishing.

Following a careful pre-polish, Loren applies 50,000 diamond compound on the clean lap. It's essential that the lap be clean. Alcohol can be used, but so can plain soap and water and a bit of elbow grease. Every other time the stone is lifted for an inspection, Loren lets a little water drip onto the lap.

Yes, the water removes the paste but not enough that it becomes too wasteful or costly.

A couple more tips on ceramic laps: before tightening down the lock nut over a ceramic lap, slip a thick piece of paper (such as from a desk blotter) about 2.5" in diameter over the lap. This way you can't tighten the lap too tightly and cause the lap to break.

Master Gemcutting Tips

Resurfacing Laps...

If you're a faceter, resurfacing a lap isn't all that difficult.

Use an old Phillips-head screwdiver or (for wax) an old aluminum dopstick. File the screwdriver or the top of the dopstick to a sharp square shape.

Use a rig from the faceting head and shave the wax or top surface off clean and flat...just a little at a time. Use very light pressure to assure an even finish. This approach works well on a copper or other soft metal lap.

You'll get best results if you don't hand hold the quill. There's too much variation in hand pressure to do a good job. A weight or rubber band will come in handy here.

Solving Difficult Polishing Problems . . .

Ever have trouble polishing peridot, enstatite, lazulite, diopside, sinhalite, kornerupine—or any other gem types containing magnesium?

Ever wonder why these particular gems are the ones that constantly pose such aggravating polishing challenges?

The answer is already provided: it's the magnesium. These stones are neutrally alkaline because of their magnesium content. What's desired is a PH factor that is either high or low, not neutral.

Test after test shows that when a gem surface has neutral PH the stone won't polish as well. That's why vinegar and diluted acid solutions mixed with the drip water prove so effective. The acid changes the PH factor, lowering it at the surface so the stone will polish instead.

Master Gemcutting Tips

When you mix a little vinegar in with some synthetic tin oxide you have an outstanding peridot polish. When the PH factor is elevated or reduced the polishing action improves dramatically. Colloidal silica is a exception: it already possesses a PH of 10-12 and with this high PH the chemical provides superior polishing capability.

The chemical action that actually takes place is this: the water and acid have low PH and this increases the hydrogen concentration. Hydrogen aggravates dislocation ie., fractures related to ductile hardening of the material. The result is more rapid removal—microscopic to be sure—of material which produces the desired polish.

The validity of this phenomenon was shown in a series of timed experiments run by Arizona's Clint Fruitman. Each run was for one minute and consisted of 180 diamond grit against sapphire. The speed of the lap was two meters per second with 22 pounds per square inch on 1(2) centimeter. What clearly comes through in these experiments is the impact of PH on removal.

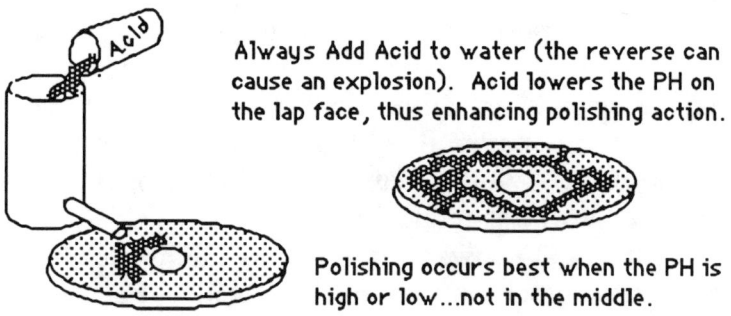

Always Add Acid to water (the reverse can cause an explosion). Acid lowers the PH on the lap face, thus enhancing polishing action.

Polishing occurs best when the PH is high or low...not in the middle.

With a PH factor of "0" some 15 milligrams were removed. When the PH was at 9—regarded as the isoelectric point or completely neutral—only 12 milligrams were removed. At high PH, the removal went back to 14.

What do these timed runs prove? Only that higher PH extremes tend to influence removal, but it's the extremes that really encourage polishing.

Techniques For Cutting Sunstone . . .

Many gemcutters, searching for a new experience, are turning to carving and sculpturing. It's a marvelous outlet for creative expression—and surprisingly enough—isn't all that difficult of a transition. Not difficult, that is, for those with some experience with stones.

One material that lends itself beautifully to carving is sunstone. This exciting member of the feldspar group is not all that familiar to many gemcutters. New finds in Idaho and Oregon may change the role of sunstone in the lapidary business.

The new sunstones coming out of these recently developed mines are exhibiting marvelous hues of red and gold. Some of the reds are nearly as bright as corundum. Internationally renowned sculptor Henry Hunt, of Arizona, is particularly fascinated with sunstone.

In his well-known book, *"Lapidary Carving For Creative Jewelry,"* Henry describes some of the features of working with sunstone.

First, its tough but soft personality makes it an easy mineral for grinding and shaping. One inch abrasive wheels work nicely on sunstone. Of course, sunstone is subject to shock and heat damage so it is important that the work be kept cool and that all cutting wheels be free of

Master Gemcutting Tips

Orientation of a sunstone is critical. Run the cleavage plane lengthwise along the longest dimension. This tip minimizes any difficulties the cleavage may offer. A good color tip: keep the stone chunky.

bumps.

So long as you remember that overheating a sunstone is an open invitation to opening up its cleavage plane you won't run into too much trouble.

Obviously you run the greatest heat danger during polish. For a first venture into carving sunstone, remove all the protuberances and visible external splits and cleavages. When you've shaped the stone down to its basic form free of unwanted elements, its shape should suggest some creative form for you to seek.

According to Hunt: "The natural fracturing pattern of stones have a peculiar way of following their own pattern. It may have something to do with their natural structure, the way the crystal forms, or the pressures exerted upon it as it does form."

Whatever form you finally decide on keep in mind

Master Gemcutting Tips

that it's best to keep your carving "chunky." This will retain whatever yellow or reddish hue the crystal specimen possesses. Likewise a fairly thick design, Hunt emphasizes, will produce a stone with a remarkable range of color densities. The purity of the color and the clarity of sunstone combine to offer exceptional brilliance despite the relatively low optical properties.

If you opt for a thin or small carving remember this: try to run the cleavage plane lengthwise along the longest dimensions. This will at least minimize any difficulties that cleavage can cause. Follow the natural forms that your crystal offers, using a fine abrasive wheel. As far as general grinding is concerned, sunstone seldom offers problems. It cuts quickly and easily and will respond readily to a grit of 600 in a small wheel or in a sand paper.

Use a light touch. If your touch remains light with a 600 sanding paper you can usually go directly and successfully to a good polish with cerium oxide. If your carving offers complex surfaces and even undercuts where the cerium oxide fails to produce the desired polish, reach for a 1000 grit Bruce Bar. On felt wheels, the Bruce Bar will give quick polishing results. It has a slight but not overly active abrasive action so a light touch with the polish (it keeps the heat down, too) is best.

Polishing sunstone with cerium oxide and felt requires caution. You don't want an excessive heat build-up because it will tend to cause streaking...not to mention possible cleavage problems. Make certain you keep the felt wet and the stone as cool as possible. Heavy pressure, as you know, aggravates the heat problem and wipes out moisture in the felt material. So keep your

Master Gemcutting Tips

touch light.

On the larger, flat surfaces of sunstone you must cope with the pitting and crazing that coarse grit laps produce. According to Hunt, the diamond paste and canvas pads that work so well on quartz and opal have the opposite effect on sunstone. The combination causes a definite sloughing off of the surface.

A phenolic disk will produce the same effect. The very nature of sunstone causes it to abrade unevenly and begin to spot polish unexpectedly.

Use 260 Grit...

The best way to avoid polishing problems is to take steps early that will bring the piece to a good pre-polish condition. This can be achieved by doing any rough sanding with a 260 grit wheel—with plenty of water and a light touch. Once the stone is shaped, refine it with a 600 grit wheel or belt, using a slow speed.

Again, with plenty of water and a light touch, work up the surface with a 3000 grit disk. A copious flow of water is vital at this stage to avoid any mud buildup that might be dragged past the polishing area and thus cause a scratch.

If you follow the steps carefully and in order, the 3000 grit should enable you to proceed to polish with a flat surface that is ready to polish.

When sunstone has been properly pre-polished, it will take the polish very quickly with little pressure. In the beginning, of course, you can minimize difficult polishing problems by designing out any large, flat surfaces. They're really the ones that will give you the most trouble—as any faceter working on a large sun-

Master Gemcutting Tips

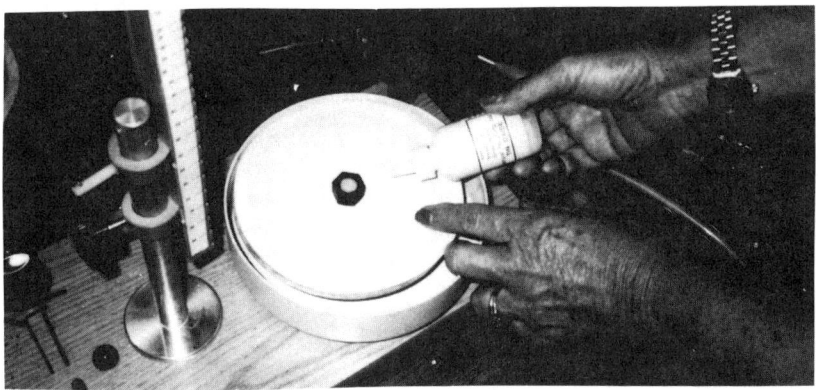

Colloidal silica enjoys a fabric-like pad so try using Pellon. This combination works well with most stones, and the Pellon retains the solution well.

stone table facet will tell you quickly.

Colloidal Silica Proves Very Effective Gemstone Polish . . .

Colloidal silica, thanks to a lack of marketing effort, is still largely unknown in the lapidary trade. Such unfamiliarity is a tragedy because the chemical is one of the best gemstone polishes available. It will bring up a fine, even polish on any gemstone short of the diamond.

That's saying a lot, but CS will actually perform that well. In 1989, *American Gemcutter Magazine,* the official publication of the American Society of Gemcutters, introduced the chemical to gemcutters.

The Society arranged for gemcutters to purchase test kits from Buehler Ltd., the Chicago based corporation which makes the product. Crystalite in Marina del Rey, CA, also produces colloidal silica. What may have initially turned off the gemcutters who bought the kit was

Master Gemcutting Tips

the polishing pads that Buehler supplied. These most definitely were not the type of polishing pads that lapidaries use and the results proved a bit less than anticipated. Plus, many gemcutters—those who are faceters—were probably unhappy because the process wasn't useful for general faceting.

It's simply outstanding for polishing a large table facet, though—if the table is the first facet cut. For faceters who for one reason or another, want to cut the table first, there can be no better choice than colloidal silica as the polish.

Large facets like the table are troublesome at the very least when it comes to polishing. The need to bring a large area flat-to-flat on a polishing laps can be most difficult. That's why many faceters often "walk" a table across the polishing wheel ie., polishing a little at a time and applying the cheater until the table is finished.

To polish a large cab or a facet with CS is simplicity itself. You first want a polishing pad material that will absorb liquids. This could be Pellon cloth, leather, felt, plain cloth . . . anything that will hold moisture. With a peel-off type rubber adhesive, attach the pad to a Lucite or rubber disk. Pellon on a Lucite disk works well, with leather or cloth on a rubber disk—and keep the pads well wetted. Then apply a dozen or so drops of the colloidal silica. Make certain you have plenty of CS on the lap and that it remains wet.

Series of Light Passes . . .

Just bring the table down onto the pad and give the facet—or an area on a cabochon—a series of 5-second, medium pressure passes. A couple of passes should do it. If

Master Gemcutting Tips

the gem surface has been properly pre-polished, the brilliant polish should jump out at you. The need to press the gem into the soft, saturated polishing pad creates a rounding. It's this aspect, of course, to which many faceters object...and which cabbers adore.

Just what it is that allows CS to produce such a rapid, fine polish is a unique chemical process. But the polish is equal to a 50,000 diamond grit finish.

There's another minor problem associated with CS. The chemical has a very high PH so it has the capability to cause some skin conditions. In addition to that, the chemical will crystalize out. It's fine particles can possibly penetrate open skin pores and maybe initiate some nuisance itching once the liquid turns crystal.

For these reasons, the manufacturer strongly urges users to wear rubber surgical gloves when working with CS. If cabbers use a horizontally mounted wheel there will be a certain amount of splash off involved. Cabbers thus are warned to wear a mask and safety glasses while polishing with a wet CS polishing pad.

Again: the results with CS polish are exceptional with only a few problems. It's a matter of making a trade-off, but there are few polishes that can do the fine, universal job as colloidal silica.

Carving Techniques With a Saw . . .

When a gemcutter needs to remove material for a unique shape it can often be a challenging task.

For example, if you had designed a piece of jewelry that required an outline of an animal such as a dog, you'd be facing some unique configurations. It isn't easy to get

Master Gemcutting Tips

stone removed from an inverted cut without damaging the rest of the piece.

That's where some good gem carving techniques come in handy. More so than faceters and traditional cabochon cutters, carvers or sculptors readily use different instruments to get the job done. In some cases, they use everyday hardware tools.

One of their more useful tools is the common flat tipped screwdriver. That's because it's probably the finest and most trustworthy "cleaving blade" available.

When you must remove material to release an unusual shape, do what the carver does. See the challenge as one that will submit to the saw and the screwdriver. First, draw a careful outline of the intended shape on the stone slab with a non-soluble pen or pencil. Then cut a series of saw cuts from the outer perimeter of the slab right up to the drawn outline. **Caution:** don't bring the saw cuts too close to the line. A saw blade is round. You

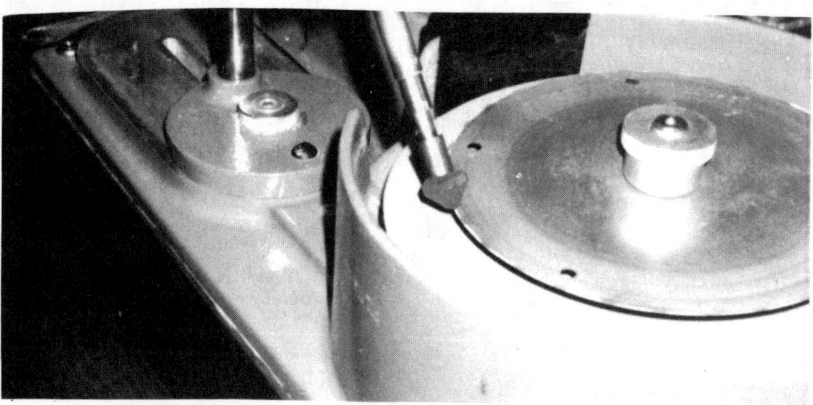

Don't overlook a saw blade on a faceting machine. It can perform outstanding gross removal while also affording you the opportunity to cut out delicate and difficult shapes. It will conserve time—and save tools.

Master Gemcutting Tips

may bring the top edge of the cut up short of the line, but the curvature of the sawblade could cut into the design.

Make a series of parallel cuts (the softer the stone the closer the cuts) all around the figure. Next, force the tip of the screwdriver between the saw cuts and wedge or lever out the sections. They will break quite easily and neatly if you're careful. Last, smooth up the outline with a cutting wheel in a lathe or small hand tool.

Paua Shells Beautiful—But Dangerous . . .

Those beautiful paua shells—scathingly defined as "airport art"—are deadly.

For gemcutters who like to work in shells, the paua represents one of the more beautiful types. This is just another reminder then. Cutting and fashioning paua shells can be very rewarding but gemcutters should keep in mind that the shell dust is "very dangerous". Breathing the tiny particles into the lungs can create serious problems, so paua dust should be viewed with the same caution as asbestos fibers.

Rule one is to use plenty of water. Keep your cutting operation wet so that dust is minimal. Don't rely on water, though. Once you cut into these shells, the cut line dries up quickly and small amounts of dust can escape.

Wear a light-weight, disposable respiration masks approved for use with asbestos while cutting paua shells. You might also make certain that a strong wind is at your back. That's one of the cautions exercised by Walter Locker, of San Francisco.

Walter actually sits in front of the family garage when cutting the paua shells. His friend, Bill Jonas,

Master Gemcutting Tips

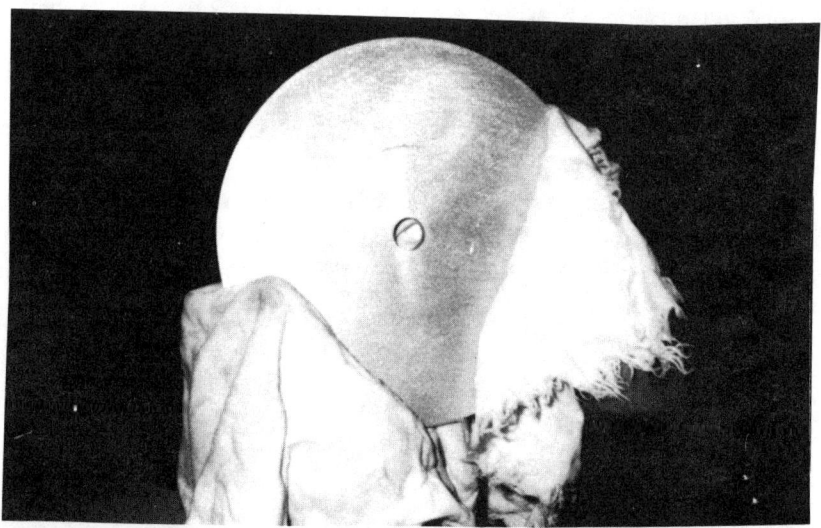

The key to scratchless gemcutting resides in clean laps and wheels. Use soap and water to clean a lap, scrub with 3M pads where warranted, and then dry off with a soft cloth. Try to store laps vertically for drip dry.

makes regular visits to Niahia Beach, CA, to get the shells. Reports are, though, that the shells aren't quite as plentiful as in the past and the findings in Wairoa, Hawke's Bay, New Zealand, are also becoming slim.

People who have handled paua without protection in the past now complain of serious respiratory problems. Therefore, if you're a novice about cutting paua shells don't work in the house without special equipment. Unless you're willing to make the investment in equipment the wisest course of action is to avoid cutting these shells. Equipment includes respirators, overalls, boots, gloves, extractor fan (or wind), and goggles.

Master Gemcutting Tips

Suggestion For Best "Universal Faceting Angles"...

A bit of a storm cloud gets kicked up by suggesting the validity of universal angles for faceting.

It was suggested that studies done by Gerald L. Wykoff, GG showed the best compromise to be an angle of 42° on the pavilion mains and 36° on the crown mains. These two angles, it was claimed, would suffice for colored stones except those where the critical angles equaled or exceeded 42°.

Thus such stones as fluorite (43°), opal (43°), scapolite (40°), feldspar (41°), quartz (at 40°), iolite (40°) might not be prime candidates for a 42° pavilion main.

As for other colored stones, the 42°-36° combination does represent the best compromise of desired faceting objectives. Defenders of traditionally recommended angles—none of whom agreed on just what constituted a "universally accepted angle combination"—took mild offense at such radicalism. There have been different angles for a long time, they insisted.

In truth, there is nothing subversive in the validity of a single set of angles. Diamond, with an RI at 2.41 is cut at 41° pavilion and 34° main. At the other extreme, we have quartz which is customarily cut at 43° pavilion and at various angles around 38°-41° crown.

Now keep in mind that there are two kinds of faceted gemstones in the world: 1) diamonds, and 2) colored stones. Whether there is agreement on this or not, these two categories represent two different cutting worlds.

In the case of diamonds, we are usually dealing with a clear or white or river colored gem crystal. It's also a crystal whose hardness varies by direction. But

Master Gemcutting Tips

the principle objective in cutting a diamond is this: we want the maximum return of white light ie., brilliance.

Only a fraction of cut diamonds—called Fancies—are cut with a color component. Even here the objective is return of white light; the color is only incidental. Seldom if ever are the traditional diamond angles altered to accommodate a better display of color.

This is not so with colored stones. The objective here is to best cut most crystals to enhance their color element. That's why they're called colored stones—even when the crystal is a clear, river hue the same as diamond. Goshenite is a white or clear beryl...but it's still regarded as a colored stone. The same holds true with silver topaz, danburite, white grossular garnet, clear quartz, white corundum: they're all colored stones.

Because a colored stone is in a category by itself, the gemcutter's objective is plural. The gemcutter wants to cut the stone in the balanced best interest of: **a) brilliance...** yes, some return of white light is necessary to produce a level of showiness in the gem; **b) color...** a law of physics states that the longer or greater duration that light travels through a medium the more color absorption occurs. Hence the color is richer; **c) dispersion...** dispersion enjoys an inverse relationship to brilliance; increase brilliance and you decrease dispersion and vice versa. Many colored stones have relatively low dispersion anyway. It is an optical truth than the thinner crown reduces dispersion. Why then opt for angles that will further reduce whatever level of dispersion the crystal enjoys anyway; **d) cone of brilliance...** by cutting the pavilion angles too close to the critical angle or by de-

Master Gemcutting Tips

creasing crown angles the cone of brilliance is reduced (the tendency to lose optical performance as the viewing angle is turned away from normal means that low angled stones can't be tilted away from a direction parallel to the viewer's eye without serious light loss eg, fisheye effect); **e) washout...** with a maximum of white light emptied through the culet and the depth of the stone minimized, the danger of color washout looms greatly.

Angles For Quartz

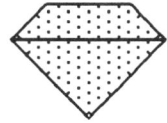 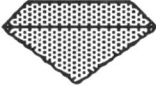 

Traditional	Wykoff*	Long/Steele
Crown 42°	36°	26°
Pavilion 43°	42°	39°

*Universal angle, applicable to any crystal

Here are some important concepts to keep in mind:

Dispersion—steeper crown angles enhance dispersion, the display of the color spectrum (*most colored stones lack high dispersion!*).

Brilliance—lower crown angles with pavilion angles slightly above critical angle improve white light return

Scintillation—smaller, flatter star facets or star row will improve a stone's ability to "twinkle" eg., reflect light.

Color Enhancement—thicker girdles improve color.

Master Gemcutting Tips

White light will dilute the hue of a crystal which is why many gemcutters cut angles even below the critical angle in order to admit more light through excessively dark colored stones.

Multiple Goals...

From the foregoing, it should be obvious that a gemcutter staring at a colored stone on his or her dopstick is balancing off five major elements that control the beauty of the stone.

The diamond cutter is seeking one major goal: brilliance. Most of the published angles have been developed by the originator's own theoretical assumptions of what will produce the greatest brilliance in a stone.

Few of these author's have produced any evidence or mathematical reasoning that would substantiate their claims to recommended angles. The closest anyone has come to this goal recently is the ray tracing work done by Norm Steel and Bob Long, both of Seattle, WA, and by computer facet design programmer Robert Strickland of Austin, TX.

Brilliance Only...

Keep in mind, though, that their studies, computer ray tracing programs, and treatises essentially cover brilliance only. Even if the recommended angles—particularly for crown main angles—seemed low the data demonstrates the variations to achieve optimum results eg., obtaining maximum brilliance.

The other objectives in colored stone cutting were not particularly addressed. Steel and Long do acknowledge the effect of added brilliance on dispersion. The 42° pavi-

Master Gemcutting Tips

lion provides a main angle that accommodates nearly all colored stones. Many diamonds are cut at 42° and viewers are hard pressed to detect the brilliance difference. Impact on dispersion is negligible The general rule of thumb holds that to decrease a pavilion angle by one degree, the crown main must be increased by two. This may be valid. Steel and Long showed it not to be the case.

36° Returns 90%...

As for a 36° crown main angle, this angle produces a light return of between 85% and 90%—if all rays are seen as entering the stone from the 90° to the table angle. This seems to show that the brilliance factor is well served at 41°-36° while at the same time a slightly thicker stone enhances color, maintains dispersion even if at a low level, and provides for a finished cut that can be tilted away from normal and still offer good optical performance.

As for the truly low refractive gems which have little talent anyway for producing brilliance, apex table facets may be the only legitimate response. This way traditional brilliance isn't demanded of the stone which is free to offer what it can in the way of scintillation, color, dispersion, and a maximum cone of brilliance. You can't completely fisheye an apex cut stone even if you reduce pavilion and crown angles dramatically. At best you may get partial fisheye effects, through some of the small facets that impose critical angle penalties on the opposite facets.

Ray Trace Evidence...

The illustrations given in this article compare ray traces between convention angles, particularly the "bril-

Master Gemcutting Tips

liant" angles offered recently by Long and Steele, and a universal 42°-36° angle set.

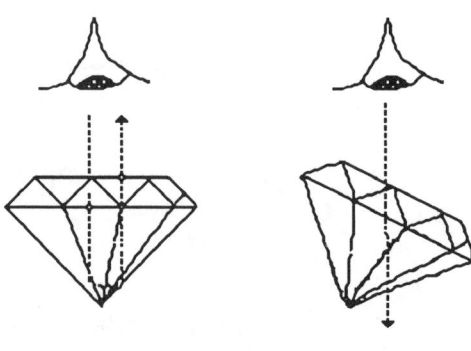

So that the reader could develop a better appreciation of the arguments, a round brilliant is used in the straight table up viewing position and in a 15° tilt from vertical. The latter is intended to show impact of the various angles on the "cone of brilliance" ie., do the angles and cut still perform optically when the stone is tilted away from the eye?

Brilliance High..

Note that in both orientations the brilliance factor of the Long and Steele recommendations of crown 27° and pavilion 40° does indeed return more light rays. In the upright and the tilted stance, a 1.54 RI stone returns all four rays examined. The T(table) S(star) M (Main) and B (Break) facets all enter the stone and return through the crown.

Master Gemcutting Tips

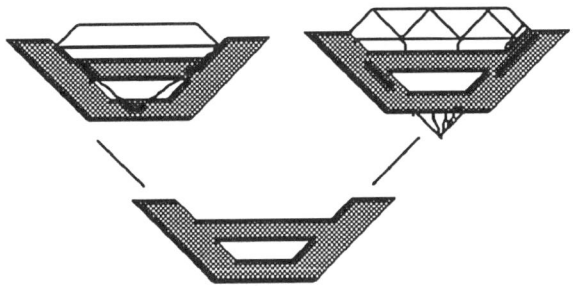

With commercial mountings, shallow stones fail to hold against the metal, thus are held only by prong legs. Large pavilion, of course, protrudes from the bottom of the mounting itself.

In the 42°-36° universal angle set, the break facet rays in both orientations are diminished somewhat. But the universal standard does return greater light activity through the table when the stone is tilted 15° off the vertical.

The traditional quartz angle recommendations of a 42° crown main and a 43° pavilion main show how poorly a traditional round brilliant performs. Light entering the crown from the mains and breaks are lost through the pavilion in a table up position. The loss is even greater when the cut is tilted 15°. In the latter case, only light entering the edges of the table are returned.

While the Long and Steele angles for maximum brilliance suggest better brightness performance, other factors need to be considered. That is, in colored stones the hue is improved by greater depth. For this reason, the 36°-42° combination appears to be a reasonable compro-

Master Gemcutting Tips

mise.

This set of angles will lose some of the light entered from the break facets near the girdle, but the thicker crown and overall greater depth of the cut improves color—and actually gathers more light because of the larger surface area of the crown facets themselves.

Breaking the Superglue Bond . . .

Having trouble breaking down the bond with superglue?

Many gemcutters find ways to contribute to the language when they try to breakdown a bond that doesn't want to break.

Well, here's an excellent method:

When you dop the stone, after the initial application has set up run a bead around the dopstick where it meets the stone. Using this procedure you'll have less than 1% of your stones come off of the dopstick, even if you're a real white knuckle polisher.

The usual complaint against using superglue is that "...it's (superglue) role in transferring is debatable because of the difficulty of removing a firm bond without adequate exposure to a strong solvent." The remedy for this is: why use a solvent at all, once the transfer has been accomplished using glue (don't forget the bead around the dopstick). Use a torch to remove the first dopstick the same way it is used to remove a wax transfer.

It will require more heat but it works (even transferring when cutting opal. Care should be used so that the heat is not applied all at once but gently by putting the torch to the dopstick and taking it away. Repeat until the

Master Gemcutting Tips

dopstick falls off. Be sure to have something that is heat resistant for the dopstick to fall onto as it gets very hot.

Special Techniques For Cabochons . . .

Think of it.

If you entered a cabochon cutting contest in Australia, your stone would be judged on 24 different items. That's for a standard cabochon, too. To the Aussie, the start of a winning cabochon starts with the slab. It absolutely must be parallel, an even thickness. Of course, if the slab is a bit off in parallelism a winning cabochon can still be attained, but the extra work doesn't justify the lack of a good slab in the first place.

The second most important approach before cutting is to check any template you plan on using. Surprisingly enough, most plastic and metal templates are highly inaccurate. This error is aggravated by the use of the pencil or aluminum pen used to scribe a cabochon outline. If you use a poorly calibrated template and then are even

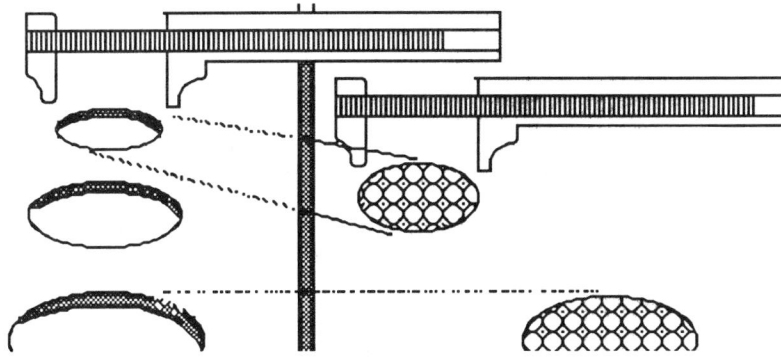

Make sure you check the template for accuracy! Most templates are highly inaccurate, particularly the metal ones.

Master Gemcutting Tips

a smidgin careless in marking the template your cabochon is wrong to begin with. So check the inside measurements of the template. Be sure to tilt the marking pencil carefully toward the inside as you scribe.

Bulk Removal With Trim Saw...

Trim sawing close to the scribed outlined allows quick bulk removal of material. It's also a good idea to use the screwdriver technique for cutting away excess mineral. This is achieved by making a series of parallel cuts—well short of the actual outline—with the saw blade. Slip the tip of a screwdriver into the saw cuts and then leverage a break out of the adjoining sections of stone. The small pieces of mineral will break off neatly up to the saw cut end. The remainder of the material around the marked line can be ground off with a coarse cutting wheel.

Once the outline shape of the cabochon has been reached the cab blank must now be checked for accuracy of its shape. Keep in mind that it's virtually impossible to cut a perfect circle but easy for a judge to assess your

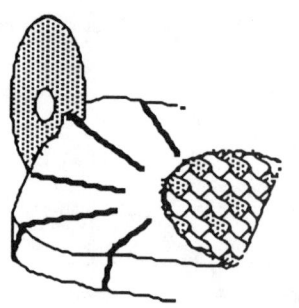
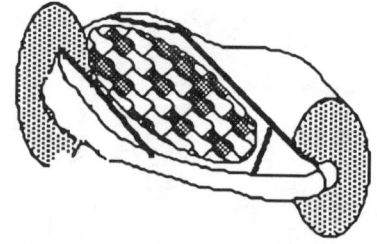

Always use the saw for easy bulk removal. It saves on laps and wheels

Master Gemcutting Tips

shortcomings. A caliper is the tool.

Tougher on Ovals...

For oval shapes, it's much tougher for a judge to discount on the plan shape because the measurements vary. That's a good point to remember when you're cutting a competition stone.

To check the accuracy of your cab blank, place it base down on a piece of white paper. Trace the outline on the paper with a fine, sharp lead pencil. The next step is to lift the stone and turn it 180 degrees. Now place the stone back down on the penciled silhouette.

Does the stone still fit the outline accurately? This is a good method to determine if your cutting has been disciplined. Indeed, try using another pencil line and drawing again. The two shapes should overlap perfectly. Any place the line deviates from the original line shows a lack of symmetry. Mark those areas where the overlap is not perfect. They need to be corrected at the next grinding step. It's best to use a finer grit when touching up. You don't want to cut too fast at this stage. Undercutting

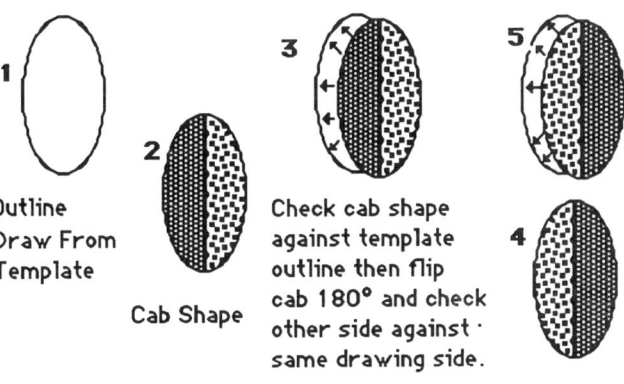

Master Gemcutting Tips

is acceptable: overcutting is ruinous.

You may have to continue the procedure of tracing your cab blank on the paper a number of times before you get a precise stone. It takes a bit of time, but a disciplined cabochon is the result—so long as the cabochon is symmetrical. Free form cabochons are something else.

Once you have the shape ground out to your satisfaction, flat lap the back of the stone. You want to remove any small chips that developed from sawing or grinding. Use a flat lap for this work. You just can't get accurate results any other way even on a vertical sanding disc. You can check your work by cross hatching (that's where you simply pencil in two sets of lines that are diagonally opposed so that all lines must disappear simultaneously to show a flat surface). The back should have a 600 grit finish at a minimum and any chips should be smaller than the intended bevel.

For marking the girdle, make certain you have a

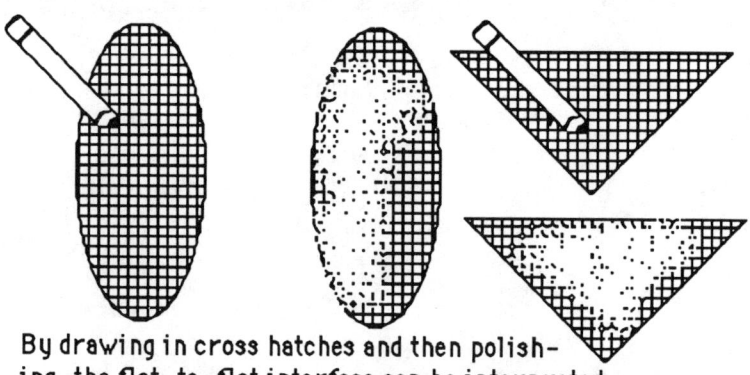

By drawing in cross hatches and then polishing, the flat-to-flat interface can be interpreted.

Cross hatching on the stone's surface—where you draw one set of lines perpendicular to another set--allows you to check on grinding and sanding. The idea is to sand or grind off all the cross hatched lines.

Master Gemcutting Tips

flat, clean table surface. To guard against scratching the just finished cab back, place a sheet of paper between the cab back and the table top. Most experienced gemcutters use a 1/16" diameter brass or aluminum rod or wire sharpened to a point as a girdle marker. A simple pencil will also do.

This will give a girdle line mark about 1/32" (about .75mm) above the table surface. A girdle line of this height will enable you to have a small back bevel of around .5mm with a setting bevel of about the same size.

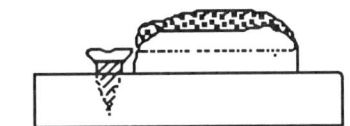
An aluminum screw in a flat piece of wood makes an excellent girdle marker

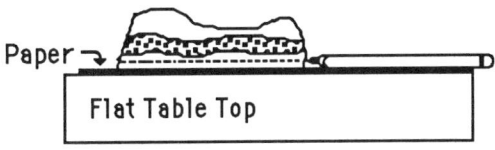
Hold the aluminum pen flat to the table and spin the cab blank around its tip.

Many gemcutters dispense with a setting bevel. Others at least allow for it in case a small girdle error creeps into the work and they need extra material to straighten up the line or remove the defect. Also, a setting bevel is welcomed by any experienced gem setter. It allows a bezel or prong to be turned down neatly over the stone's edge.

Slope is Critical...

The critical stage of cabochon cutting comes down to the control of the slope from the apex to the girdle. Grind

Master Gemcutting Tips

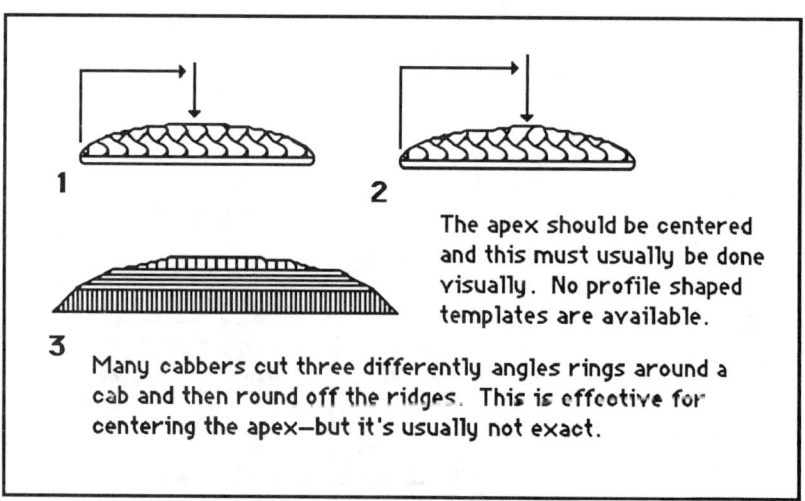

down the top of your cabochon to an even curve, bringing the curvature down to the girdle line. This is where the slightest miscalculation makes you happy that you planned earlier for a setting bevel. Any not-too-serious mistake can be corrected without disfiguring the work.

How do you evaluate a cabochon top as far as disciplined roundness is concerned? Avoiding the "off center" problem isn't the easiest of gemcutting tasks when you're cutting free hand. That's the toughest assignment in cabochon cutting.

The Aussies have an answer to this challenge. It's called a "Barnett Gauge." The gauge can easily be made from two flat wooden blocks. On the base block, cover the top edge with a flat piece of Formica or plastic so you'll have a hard, flat base for the stone. The upright block features a series of 1/16" separated parallel lines that have been scribed into the surface using a draftsman's "T" square.

Master Gemcutting Tips

Remove your stone from its dopstick (if like most gemcutters you've dopped the stone rather than hand hold!) and clean it off thoroughly.

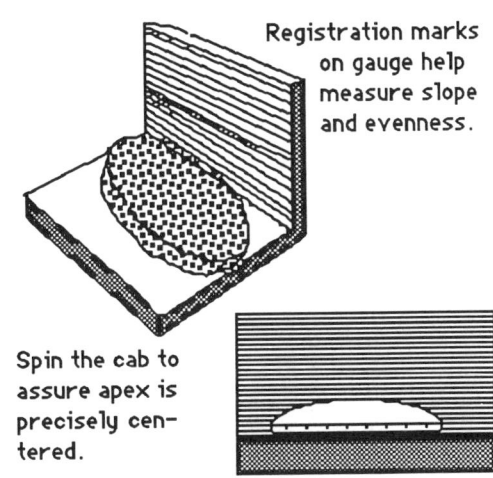

Registration marks on gauge help measure slope and evenness.

Spin the cab to assure apex is precisely centered.

Set the gauge on a reasonably flat surface at eye level. Turn the cabochon upside down and set it—rounded top down on the base block—on the gauge. It should sit level in all positions and parallel to one of the scribed lines on the back board. Take a pencil tip and spin the cabochon slowly checking the flat base against the parallel lines. There should be no deviation. The cabochon should sit on the apex of its dome and spin in a rigid parallel motion.

If it doesn't sit level as depicted in the drawing above then you'll need to grind a bit more off the high side. It goes without saying that you should persist in checking and grinding until the stone spins 360 degrees without a suggestion of wobble.

Sand With 220...

One point is important here. Before submitting your cabochon to the Barnett Gauge, it should be sanded fine with at least a 220 grit. If the stone passes the gauge examination, you're ready to dop back up for pre- and final polishing.

Master Gemcutting Tips

Here's a cabochon cutting tip from a Supreme Master: take your grinding up through pre-polish with diamond grit. For example, proceed 325, 600 and 1200. Check between each sanding step with a 10x magnifier. At 1200 there should be NO residual scratches.

Go to cerium oxide for the final polish—but only after you've absolutely assured yourself that the 1200 diamond re-polish was immaculate. The reason for cerium oxide is this: tin oxide leaves tiny scratches that are perfectly all right for commercial cutting but could be detected by a sharp eyed competition judge.

Furthermore, the better the pre-polish the less time must be spent in polishing. Excessive polishing is quite dangerous to the stone's surface because it introduces overcutting and pits.

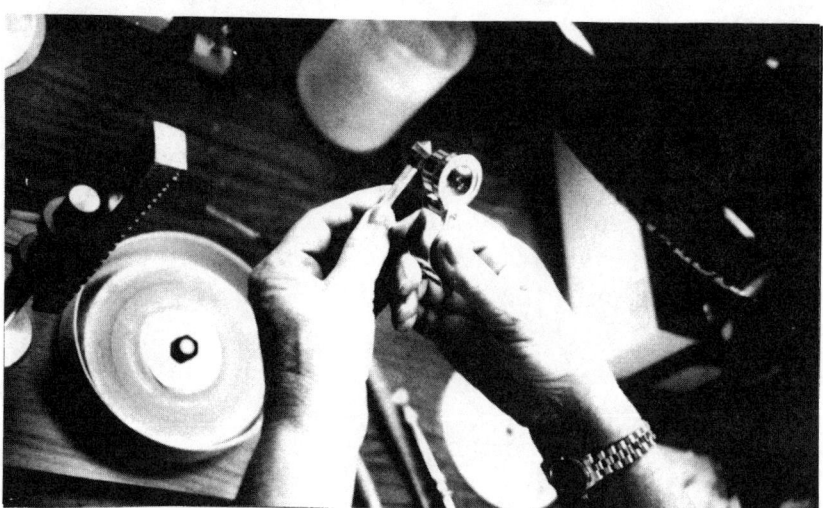

Whether faceting or cabbing, check the pre-polish thoroughly. Absence of all scratches assures a superior polish. A 1200 pre-polish is fine for most gemstones but use 3000 on harder gems, those over 8 MOHS.

Master Gemcutting Tips

The final check should be made with a 10x magnifier under at least a 40 or 60 watt incandescent unfrosted bulb. It's better to check under a 100 or 150 watt bulb. These brighter lamps will reveal conditions you can only guess at with the lower wattage bulbs...although remember that they burn much hotter.

With the top finished, the stone should be re-dopped so you can work the base and the bevel. Use only new wax when dopping on your newly polished surface. Old wax can possibly introduce contaminants that scratch.

Use nothing coarser than 325 on the base or bevels lest you misshape them. If the base does need some extra grinding, say a 600 grit, don't use a wheel. Drop some loose silicon carbide 600 grit on a plate of glass and hand lap. Flatness can be checked with the gauge or an engineer's 6-inch straight edge.

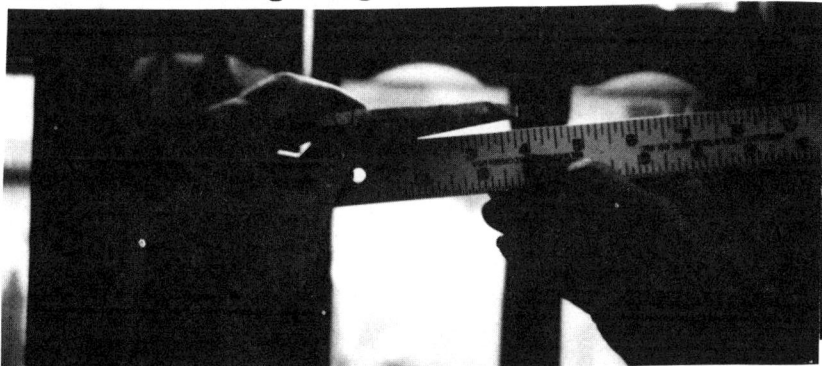

A gauge or engineer's straight edge when held flush across the bottom of a cabochon allows you to make a visual check to assure true flatness.

Finish the back off using a good, strong light and move the stone in all directions. You'll find scratches better this way. You must find the scratches at this

Master Gemcutting Tips

To obtain a flat cabochon back use a faceter's pre-polish lap or place 1200 diamond paste on a master lap and work slowly for a smooth, even finish.

stage. If not, you'll certainly discover them on final polish.

The pre-polish can be handled a couple of ways. If you're lapping with 600 grit on glass, stop adding new grit while you sand. The particles will usually break down even under modest pressure if you add only water and you'll end up with something close to a 1000 finish.

Or, use either a 1200 bonded lap similar to the ones used by faceters or place some 1200 diamond paste on a flat lap. Lock the stone to the lap: don't try to hand hold it. This will give you a tremendous pre-polish. It means less polishing time which is what every gemcutter wants in the final stage. To cut the bevel, keep in mind that a back bevel should be between 45° and 70° from the horizontal. Edges should be clearly defined and no less than 20% of the thickness of the stone.

You can attain a bevel this accurate with a fine diamond lap or even a hard backed vertical sanding disc. Hold the dopstick at the required angle and make no less than four passes to cut the girdle. Keep the disc wet and

Master Gemcutting Tips

work slowly—and with light pressure. You don't need to cut the entire girdle in the first pass. Besides, it would probably be disfigured if you did anyway owing to unequal hand pressure.

Try to maintain the same angle to avoid steps in the bevel's width. Once you've cut the bevel, lightly sand it with 1200. The emphasis is on the word "lightly." A bevel is generally quite small and any excessive pressure will produce odd results in the girdle line.

As for polishing, again use absolutely no more than necessary pressure to get the scratch free finish you desire. Before going on to the next step, check the work just finished with a good light and a 10x magnifier.

When the magnifier—and your eye—shows the stone is finished, pop it in the refrigerator (if you're using dopping wax which would be the safest adhesive when attaching a dopstick to a polished dome).

In a few moments the cab will break free. Give it a good alcohol cleaning with a nice, soft and very clean rag.

Quick Sawing...

How do you get rid of the bulk of a facetable stone and still achieve a respectable yield?

Faceter F. E. Keller, of Gilbert, AZ, puzzled over that one. He came up with this ingenious response:

Put a large steel washer as a spacer on the spindle of your faceting machine, atop a regular girdling lap. Then lock down a diamond cut-off saw blade over the spacer.

With careful adjustments to your machine's faceting controls, saw away the bulk. This saves large sections of

Master Gemcutting Tips

cutting material for later use, reduces the wear and tear on your grinding laps and speeds up removal and control by a large factor.

If you do the sawing carefully and with a plan there's often very little pre-forming left to do...and you have perhaps a handful of perfectly good faceting material for cutting other stones.

Use of Epoxy...

Dopping remains a problem—and a controversy. Not for Donald P. Richardson, of Do-Re Gemcraft, Lake City, FL.

Don has been using quick-hardening epoxies since the early 70s and it's been years since he's had a stone pop off the dopstick whether faceting or cabbing.

In faceting, he uses the same epoxy for the initial dopstick as he does for the transfer. In the latter case,

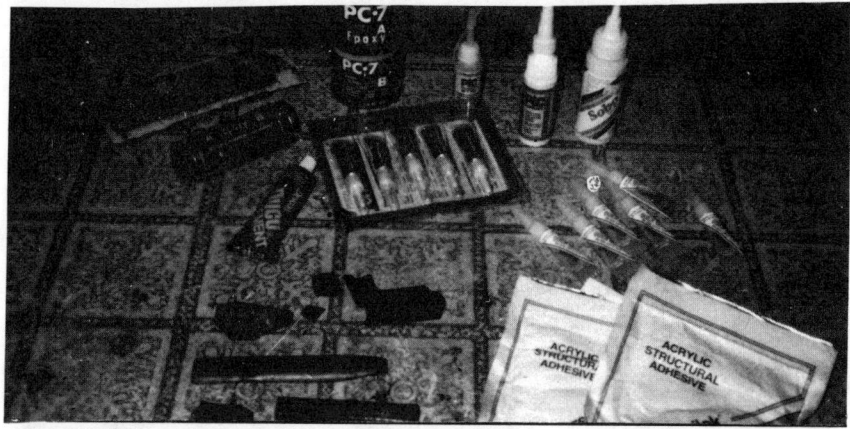

Even with a variety of adhesives to choose from, fast-setting two-part epoxy is gradually becoming the preferred dopping material for many gemcutters.

Master Gemcutting Tips

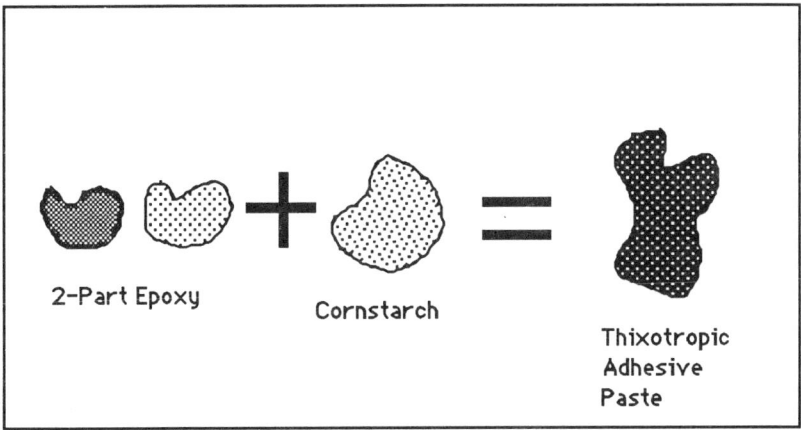

though, he adds a little cornstarch to the dop epoxy in case he later decides to soak off the completed stone in Attack.

[Editor's Note: Cornstarch also adds a bit of thixotropicity to the epoxy. That's a fancy word for saying that the epoxy won't be as runny, that it will hold its formed shape even in a vertical application. When a resin will do this it's said to be "thixotropic."]

In setting the initial dopstick, Don makes sure that the epoxy is mixed in exact portions so that it always sets very "hard." He doesn't allow the dopstick to touch the stone either, making certain that a thin layer of paper separates the two.

There's a method in his madness for separation. Before removing the stone and dopsticks from the fixture after transfer, Don carefully saws through the epoxy of the initial dopstick with a fine jeweler's saw blade. In a matter of seconds he's ready to start cutting again on the opposite side of the stone—after making absolutely certain that the epoxy has hardened.

Master Gemcutting Tips

The only problem that you'll probably encounter with the Richardson idea is when you don't mix the epoxy in proper proportions. Then it won't harden properly.

Cutting Grooves and Channels . . .

Carving grooved or channeled forms in gemstones is one of those extra skills that many gemcutters are seeking.

As more and more designers look for faceted stones and cabochons which reflect the contemporary geometric channeling ie., illusion cutting, gemcutters find they must get with the flow.

Cutting channels is not all that difficult. It's actually quite simple. But getting a commercially acceptable polish on the channels can be very difficult...unless—!

Sometimes, if the cutting is done improperly it is virtually impossible to achieve a good polish.

When a gemcutter develops truly effective carving skills he or she will be able to perform concave, convex, flats, undercuts, recessed and hollowed out cuts. These are talents not easily acquired but with effort and practice you can soon be cutting marvelously contemporary designs.

Designing Carvings...

If a gemstone creation is to have numerous grooves and channels, it is best to proceed from a firm design. Some experienced cutters, of course, can design as they proceed but it's still best to have a design goal in mind.

According to famed sculptor Henry Hunt, any stone shape is best if one side is slightly wider than the others

Master Gemcutting Tips

in order to give the ultimate work a finished face. He dislikes squaring up any stone because it has a tendency to round off into a cylinder.

Most gemcutters will find that either cabochon technique or pre-form faceting can produce the initial shape. Faceting tends to produce sharp corners or face (facet) edges. Once you have a basic shape, the major channels

or grooves can be made using the dressed corners of a silicon carbide wheel. Make certain the corners are truly dressed with a diamond dresser.

Earlier it was emphasized that cutting channels isn't difficult: polishing improperly cut channels is a serious problem. When you cut a channel in a gemstone, it should be a single, smooth cutting motion. By making single, disciplined channel cuts you impart a smooth homogenous surface to the channel walls. This kind of

Master Gemcutting Tips

smooth surface makes it possible for you to achieve a good pre-polish. If you cut with a fine enough grit you can almost go directly to final polish.

If you make the original channel cuts with a series of short, individual cutting passes you create a series of different angled facets to the walls. It's very difficult and sometimes impossible to pre-polish these different planes.

Can you cut rough channels and still get a pre-polish? The answer is "yes." If you have rough, multi-planed channels, the only way to prepare them for polish is to cut away the roughness and facet edges with small diamond tips. This is a longer much more complex process but sometimes, particularly for difficult channels, it is the only way to proceed.

Most of the time, the corner of the wheel will be able to produce the size channel you want. If you do want a wider groove, make two parallel passes on the wheel

The edge of a silicon carbide wheel can be properly dressed and then used to cut the channels that characterize the new fantasy cuts.

Master Gemcutting Tips

edge, or on a smaller appropriately sized flat edged wheel. Break out the middle ridge of wide channels with a screwdriver or sharp chisel.

Yes, many gemcutters do all of their channeling on the corner of a 220 silicon carbide wheel. But if you wish different configurations it will be necessary to change to small cutting wheels.

In *American Gemcutter Magazine,* instructions were given for making a small one-inch diamond carving wheels out of silicon carbide, buttons, etc. These are the wheels that truly allow a gemcutter to achieve intricate carvings. To be sure, if you are cutting with small wheels of 220-325 grit the channels will be left sandy. But small wheels do allow much greater control.

When you are finished channeling with the small cutting wheels, select a tapered diamond tip or a shaped small silicone abrasive wheel and begin cleaning up and refining the small grooves first. Work slowly and make certain that any different planes are smoothed off. A final step would be to use a larger diamond wheel and refine any bottoms in the larger channels and areas.

Once this initial cleanup has been finished, many carvers go to sanding grits of 400 and 600 grit. On areas of any size this can be a long, arduous process. When you have achieved a dull sheen on the stone's surface it's ready for polish.

It may sound like carping, but it's still much easier to cut smooth channels, dress them up with a small abrasive wheel and then go to polish. The great benefit of fine grit silicone abrasive wheels—the kind used in dentistry (not rubber abrasive wheels because they'll leave a residue and a wavy surface on the stone that is most dif-

Master Gemcutting Tips

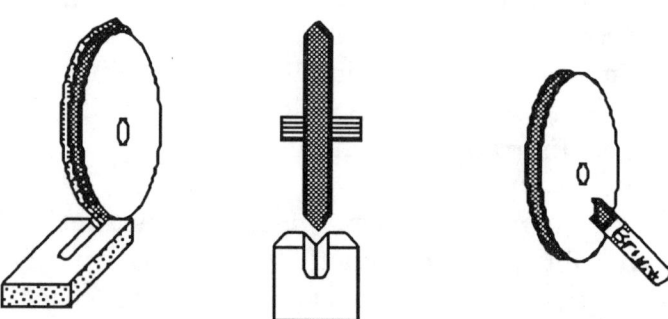

Use a felt polishing wheel on all fantasy cuts made of minerals that do not seriously undercut. A Bruce Bar is handy for dispensing polish.

ficult to correct or polish)is that they can also be used to dress up other surfaces on the stone itself.

Once you've got a smooth finish on all surfaces, go to a a large or small felt wheel (unless the mineral undercuts) for a chemical polish. Depending on the stone's MOHS hardness, use a chemical polish such as cerium oxide (quartz, garnet, etc.) or Linde A (topaz, tourmaline, beryl). An an alternative to a paste, try a convenient Bruce Bar.

As you proceed with the polish, you'll no doubt see areas or spots where the pre-polishing was inadequate. This is the moment of decision for any gemcutter: do you stop polishing and return to the fine sanding or do you go ahead. Yes, very fine scratches might be ignored. Only you can decide on more noticeable shortcomings.

On large, broad surfaces of the stone use a large felt wheel. Opt for the small wheels for the small channels.

Master Gemcutting Tips

Don't spend excessive time on the polishing wheels. After all, polishing is an abrading process and constantly poses the danger of rounding off sharp edges. Spend extra time at pre-polish: that's really where the secret of any fine—and quick—polish resides. Not until you have ALL the scratches and imperfections from the sanding operations removed should you move on to polishing.

Once you obtain the polish, that's it. Additional time spent on a felt polishing wheel will not improve the polish but it will tend to round off the channel edges. On these new contemporary cuts, you don't necessarily want or need extremely sharp edges or corners but you do want them distinct.

Lap Tips From Experts . . .

In faceting the whole concept calls for using the lap

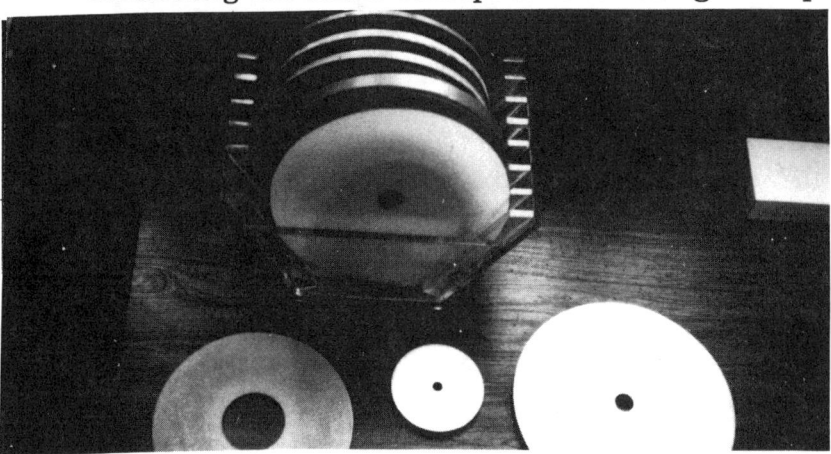

Many gemcutters have a wide variety of laps and wheels but faceting requires only 2-3 laps and cabbing needs only about a half dozen.

Master Gemcutting Tips

that best does the job.

For example, a 260 diamond grit lap should usually be reserved strictly for preforming and for main facets on very large stones. A new metal bonded 260 grit wheel or lap is highly aggressive. Invariably leaves very deep scratches. Such scratching requires a considerable cutting allowance for prepolishing with the 1200 grit wheel. The proper allowance can be most difficult for the beginner to estimate.

Until you have a feel for the cutting speed of your laps, try using the 600 for cutting large facets. It also has a relatively rapid cutting action but leaves a much smoother surface for prepolishing. The beginner can cut close to the final facet size.

Nearly every experienced faceter prefers the 1200 lap—often even a 3000 grit lap—to be used for all small facets. Remember that a 1200 cuts quickly enough but generally leaves a surface which can be taken to polish, but with difficulty. This is where the phenolic comes in.

Use a phenolic lap with 3000 diamond compound—or a 3000 grit lap (a resin bonded 3000 lap is great for prepolishing and cutting tiny facets because it tends to cut a bit slower than a metal bonded lap)...after the 1200. The result is a very high prepolish, easily seen, and easily brought to a final polish. It is a versatile lap and produces a flat surface. It has particular value in polishing corundum. This saves wear and tear on a 3000 diamond lap...[but remain wary] this 3000 has some cutting action so care must still be exercised.

The plain iron lap can be used to polish stones harder than quartz. Many professional faceters use iron with 100,000 diamond compound to polish garnet, peridot, to-

Master Gemcutting Tips

paz, CZ, beryl, and corundum...it produces a very flat facet and an excellent polish. It should be used at a very slow speed...apply a very little amount of diamond, spread it with your finger using a little olive oil and then wipe it with tissue while running at low speed...use spray diamond sparingly, but still wipe it a bit with a tissue. Too much diamond causes scratches and so will excessive speed.

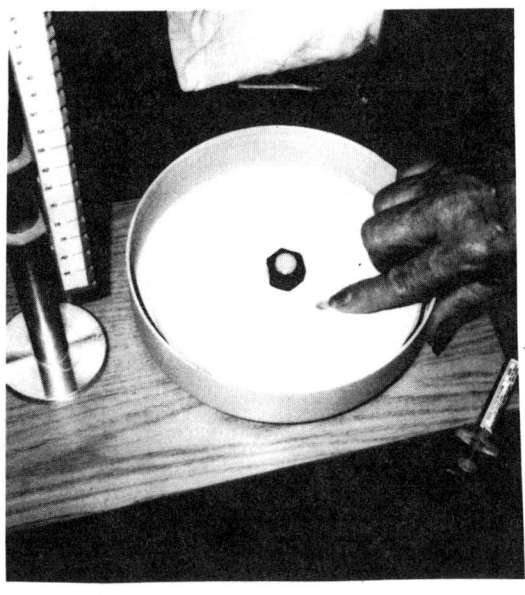

It's also a good idea to use the Lucite lap with cerium oxide for quartz. The other side of the lap can be used with tin oxide for glass.

Constructing a 1/10 Vernier . . .

For faceters whose machines aren't equipped with a 1/10 degree vernier the problem isn't all that great.

You can easily make your own. Hugh M. Rackets of Houston, TX, offers the following steps (and drawing):

1. In order to divide one degree into ten equal parts it requires an arc of nine degrees.

2. Determine the number of degrees required to make one revolution of your machine.

Master Gemcutting Tips

3. Divide this number into 360 degrees. This gives the ratio. (Mine is 360/60 equals 6 therefore a ratio of 6 to 1).

4. Lay out an arc of 9 degrees X your ratio to any convenient scale. (Mine is 9 x 6 equals 54 degrees.)

5. Measure the radius of the protractor on your machine. (Mine is 2.5cm.)

6. Draw this radius on your arc as shown.

7. Divide large arc into 10 equal by trial and error.

8. Place a gummed label over the subscribed arc-radius of your protractor.

9. Mark the gummed label as shown.

10. Remove the label, cut on the radii as shown, and place on your machine.

Making Your Own Laps . . .

Laps can be expensive, regardless of whether

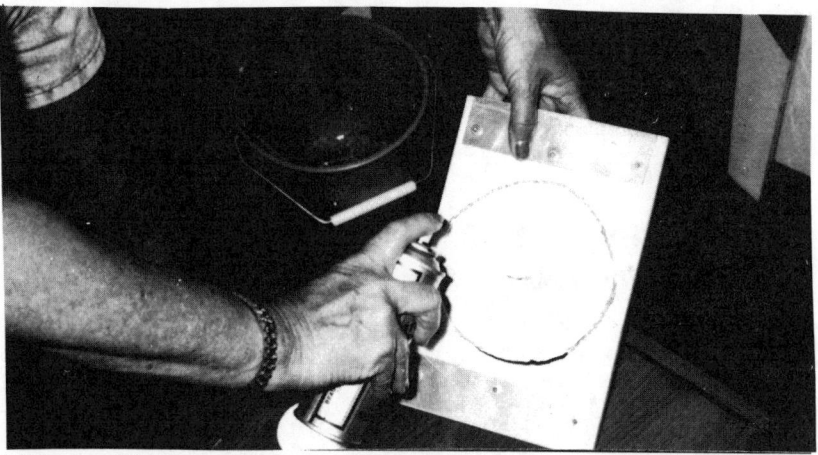

It takes a little patience but no great insight or talent to make your own laps, just a few items that can be purchased in any hardware store...a plastic disk, some spray paint and grit.

Master Gemcutting Tips

you're a cabber, carver, or faceter.

One way around this dilemma is to make your own laps. That's what the late Warren R. Morrison of Watertown, WI, did. Here's Warren's method:

"I have used Lucite, Corian, and Lexan in the plastics group, and also have melted, cast, mounted and machined several alloys containing tin, lead and antimony."

He made a small forge that uses charcoal for fuel with a blower to supply air. Temperatures easily reach 800-1000 degrees F. Molten metal is poured into a constructed mold of aluminum, a bit larger than 8 inches in diameter to a depth of about 1/4 inch. This casting is cemented with epoxy to an aluminum back and machined on an ancient Atlas milling machine to 8 inches in diameter and made flat across the lap.

"I usually end up with a lap this is 0.002 inches in variance from center hole to outer circumference edge.

"I have made about 30 laps. One alloy that is quite good is the babbitt bearings from old farm machinery of which there is a great deal in this farm area. Other alloys are purchased from local scrap dealers. Babbitt occurs as tin or lead which I separate by specific gravity using a home made specific gravity instrument described in *"In the Art of the Lapidary"* (an excellent book by Francis J. Sperisen, published in 1961).

"Antinomy is used in these laps to impart hardness to the alloy. The critical step in lap making is the machining of the surface to a fair flatness.

"I don't score the metal but do use a soluble oil solution mixed with vinegar for my polishing liquid drip. Linde A or cerium oxide are the compounds of choice.

Master Gemcutting Tips

Lap speeds are about 200 rpm except for synthetic spinel which I find polishes much easier if the speed is increased to about 700-750 rpm. Plastic laps such as Lucite and Corian run best at about 100-150 rpm."

What Every Gemcutter Should Know About Abrasives . . .

To reach and maintain a peak of lapidary skills every gemcutter should have a thorough understanding of abrasives.

They are, after all, the true fuel of lapidary. Without the abrasive action nothing would happen. All the hardware and equipment that is available in lapidary is ultimately dedicated to the maximum use of some kind of agent that will abrade or wear away mineral surfaces. That has always been the whole essence of gemcutting.

For many beginning gemcutters, though, the involvement with abrasives consists of merely putting the nearest wheel, belt, or disk on a cutting machine and flipping on the switch. The abrasive of choice among contemporary cutters is diamond, often referred to as boart, thanks to its top MOHS or hardness ranking. With a hardness rank of 10, diamond particles will scratch or abrade every other substance on earth—including diamond itself.

There is no doubt that diamond ranks as probably the finest and most universal of lapidary abrasives. Keep in mind, though, that reliance on diamond—or any of the other abrasives—as the sole abrasive agent you use can seriously limit your gemcutting accomplishments.

Certain applications can be better done using a softer

Master Gemcutting Tips

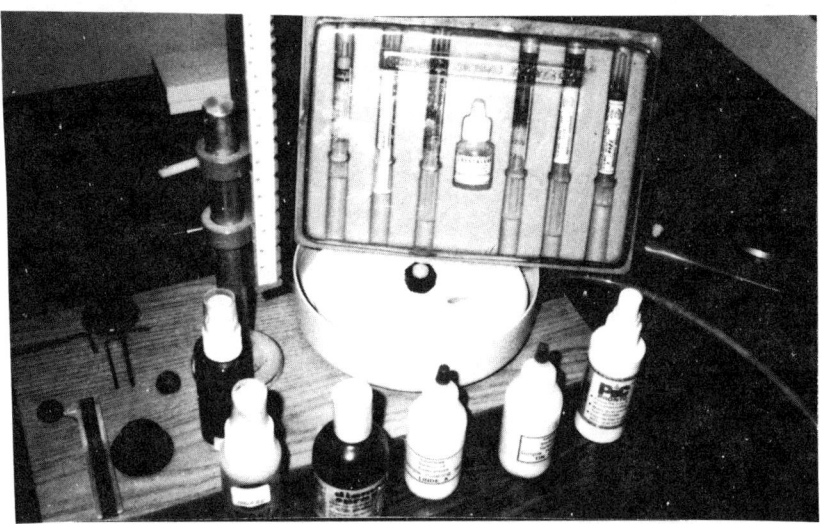

Today's gemcutters can call on a wide variety of adhesive materials for attaching stones to dopsticks e.g., dopping waxes, epoxies, cyanoacrylates, glues, sodium silicate, two-faced tape, mechanical fasteners, etc.

abrasive which exhibits different cutting action—or performs the same task with less expense. Whether natural or man-made, diamond remains the most expensive of the abrasives.

So that you will be able to make effective decisions regarding abrasives, here is a list and a description of each of the different types available. You'll note that some of the metallic oxides—better recognized as lapidary polishes—are also included. The precise chemical reaction that these polishes exert on a stone surface is still largely unknown, but there is no question whatsoever that their relative hardness are significant to polishing and that they do exert an abrasive action.

Master Gemcutting Tips

Super Abrasives
Diamond
Cubic Boron Nitride (CBN)
Boron Carbide (BC)

Standard Abrasives
Silicon Carbide
Carborundum
Emery
Silicate particles (sand)

Traditional Abrasives
Quartz (flint)
Garnet
Corundum

Polishing Abrasives
Alumina Oxide (corundum)
Tin Oxide
Chromic Oxide
Cerium Oxide

A rather impressive list, and perhaps a bit longer than you realized, isn't it?

Don't allow the number of different types to become intimidating. Some aren't used any more while others have limited applications.

Almost all abrasives are graded by number. The higher the number the finer the size of individual particles. Thus grit sizes of 220 or 400 are much coarser than 1200 or 8000.

Master Gemcutting Tips

In the rush to embrace diamond technology, many gemcutters overlook the benefits offered by silicon carbide wheels. The latter can be "dressed" into special configurations for virtually any kind of gemcutting.

Man Made Particles...

Since the turn of the century, man-made abrasives—especially silicon carbide and diamond—have proven most popular because of their availability, efficiency, and low cost.

In the past—or at least before technology provided adhesive techniques that would marry the abrasive to a cutting surface—abrasives were generally used loose. That is, they were placed in measured amounts as a graded powder or "grit" between the stone surface and a moving surface in such a way that movement would cause the abrasive to wear away the stone.

There are still many applications for loose grit. Chief among contemporary uses include tumbling, large flat work, mud type sawing, drilling, and hand lapping small pieces.

Master Gemcutting Tips

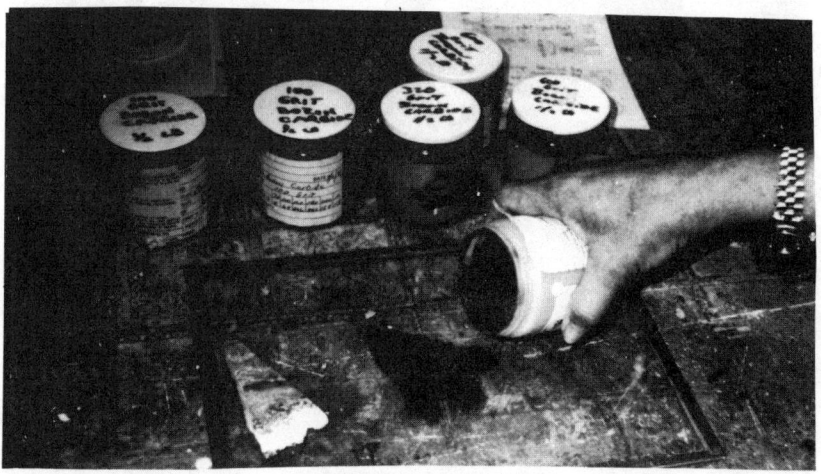

The new super abrasives can be used loose (they are superb for flat lapping) or can be mixed with an oil, paste, or bonded in resin or metal.

Super Abrasives...

At the top of the use list are the super abrasives ie., diamond, cubic boron nitride, and boron carbide.

Like most other abrasives, these exceedingly hard substances are used loose or when attached to cutting surfaces by means of resins, metal plating, sintering, or simply by "charging" ie., forcing diamond particles into a surface with pressure.

Diamond...

The hardest natural substance on earth, diamond is probably the most popular abrasive among lapidaries. It will scratch anything, including itself.

Diamond hardness varies by direction. Thus a diamond is cut or abraded by subjecting a soft grain direction against the occasional hard points of many diamond particles arranged randomly on a cast iron surface.

Master Gemcutting Tips

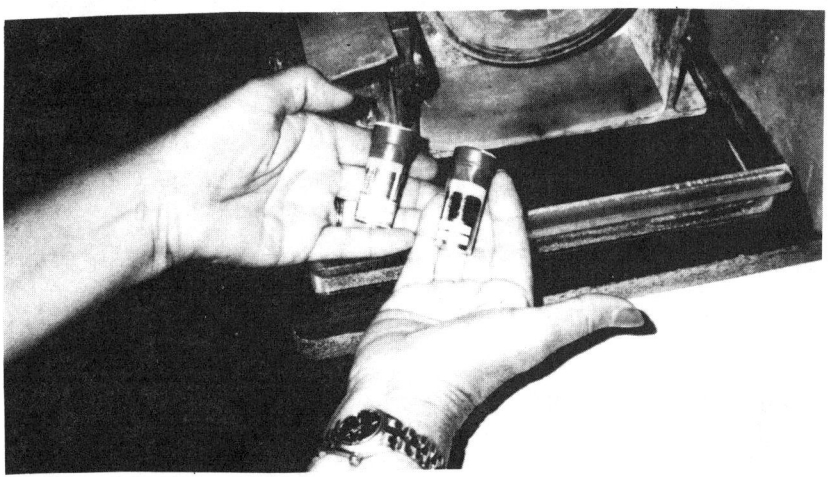

Unless you are cutting diamonds, the grain—and therefore the hardness— direction of diamond boart is irrelevant.

Most contemporary diamond cutting products contain synthetic diamond particles rather than natural material. The latter type consist of irregular shaped particles whose shards and fragments are quickly and easily broken off under the wear and tear of abrading hard materials, thus dulling somewhat the initial cutting efficiency. Man-made diamonds are more consistently blocky. While they may round off a bit through extensive use they are much less likely to break up or fragment.

Both types are highly effective both as loose particles (mostly in fine grit sizes for polishing) or when incorporated in a host range of 100 (for coarse cutting) to 100,000 (super fine polishing).

Whether for cabbing or faceting, most gemcutters using diamond prefer a 230 grit for grinding, a 1200 or 3,000 for pre-polishing and 14,000 for polishing.

Master Gemcutting Tips

Cubic Boron Nitride..

At one time, cubic boron nitride was thought to be lapidary's answer to a truly super abrasive that would be efficient, long lasting, and inexpensive.

While it is second only to diamond in hardness, CBN is little used in lapidary. It's future doesn't look particularly bright either. Why? Well, the man-made CBN is produced in consistently blocky, rounded nuggets. This kind of particle is especially effective with long fibered elements such as copper, brass, etc. Most minerals are notably short fibered with the possible exception of jade, spodumene, serpentine, etc.

Boron Carbide...

Boron Carbide (BC) is a very hard (9.57 MOHS, 2400 Knoops), highly refractory material used both as an abrasive and as an abrasion-resistant material.

When BC participles are pressed together under pressure the result is a highly abrasion-resistant surface.

As an abrasive, BC is mostly used loose, for ultrasonic grinding and drilling, fine polishing—but not usually for bonded abrasive wheels. While BC is very hard, it is also very brittle and sensitive to impact. Under normal lapidary grinding conditions, the BC particles would be subject to high impact.

A gemcutter would be interested in BC for its high and long lasting polishing qualities. For example, when hand working the close fitting parts for opal doublets or triplets, BC is a superb loose grinding and polishing performer. It is generally made into a watery slurry for lapping on glass.

Master Gemcutting Tips

BC is also effective for small flats and impact sensitive stones. The BC is hard and efficient but also breaks down into a finer slurry with use.

Make Diamond Paste . . .

You can make your own diamond paste—and save plenty of money.

The commercial syringes containing diamond mixed with a paste are expensive. No doubt about it.

Professional gemcutter Don Cook of Norfolk, NE, had no intention of paying out good money for a product he could more easily make himself. Here's how Don makes his own paste:

He uses plain old grocery store olive oil and loose diamond powder. The olive oil is purchased at the store, and the loose powder is bought cheaply in 100 carat vials.

Just add a few drops of olive oil to the diamond powder

You can easily—and inexpensively—make your own diamond paste by adding a few drops of olive oil to loose diamond powder and mixing it with your finger. The paste is then applied with the finger as needed.

Master Gemcutting Tips

Says Don, "I mix the two in a plastic teaspoon. I put 5 carats of diamond powder in the spoon and add 4-5 drops of olive oil. I mix it with my finger to a very thick slurry and then apply that in dabs with my finger, rubbing the solution over the entire surface of the lap. No big deal. I just rub it in and spread it with my finger.

"It takes only a few seconds to charge a lap and then you might have to recharge it after a stone or two. That's a small price to pay, though, for the rewards you get with diamond polishing...the inexpensive kind."

Is it worth it? Well, a pint of olive oil will last, oh, 300 years the way you'll be using it. Loose diamond boart, of course, is quite inexpensive.

You'll hear this elsewhere but don't bother with liquid detergent in place of the olive oil. You don't get good polishing results with the detergent.

Good Use For Ceramic Laps...

Don't throw away that old ceramic lap that was originally produced as a computer memory disk. It's valuable as a master lap.

Without porosity, your old computer disk isn't worth a tinker for polishing on its surface. As a master lap for Ultra Laps, though, it's found an inviting home in lapidary.

Even a porous ceramic lap should be limited in use to polishing only a few stones at a time. After 4-5 stones they'll start to scratch your stones. Ceramic laps, say experienced gemcutters, are great for working on a single competition stone—but they're lousy and unreliable as production laps. Get a good cast iron lap if you want pro-

Master Gemcutting Tips

Those old, ineffective ceramic laps—the ones lacking porosity and thus won't polish—are useful in the role of master lap for holding Ultra Laps charged with diamond. The combination makes a terrific polishing unit.

duction.

And if you want the neatest, fastest, and least troublesome polishing setup you've ever experienced, try using the combination of ceramic master lap and Ultra Lap.

Willard Augsburger of Shreveport, LA, a longtime gemcutter and teacher of electronics, came up with the idea—and pure joy—of using the ceramic lap properly. And that is: use the ceramic lap as a master lap for an Ultra Lap which is then charged with diamond. This combination will produce a polish that is incredibly quick and excellent—and no hint of edge rounding. Talk about a beautiful combination.

Now, here's Willard's genius on this idea. Use a worn out Ultra Lap and charge it with diamond paste and

Master Gemcutting Tips

To assure that the Ultra Lap will remain attached to the ceramic master lap, coat the ceramic lap with olive oil and then squeegee off with a razor blade. The Ultra Lap will stay put.

place it on the ceramic lap. First, though, and this is the key to the idea, you put olive oil on the ceramic lap as the adhesive. Wipe the olive oil on the ceramic surface with your fingers and then squeegee it back off the surface with a razor blade. Now lay the Ultra lap on the coated surface. The olive oil will grip the Ultra lap on the surface of the ceramic lap like glue—and you get the sharpest facet edges you've ever gotten with any kind of plastic lap.

To keep the Ultra Lap polishing you merely charge it with diamond paste. Yes, you can use new Ultra Laps. As a matter of fact the diamond impregnated 3M and Mayco laps make excellent polishing pads on a ceramic back.

So, don't throw away those old ceramic laps that you couldn't get to work right. They're dynamite as a master lap to hold diamond charged Ultra Laps for the best polishing combination you can imagine.

Master Gemcutting Tips

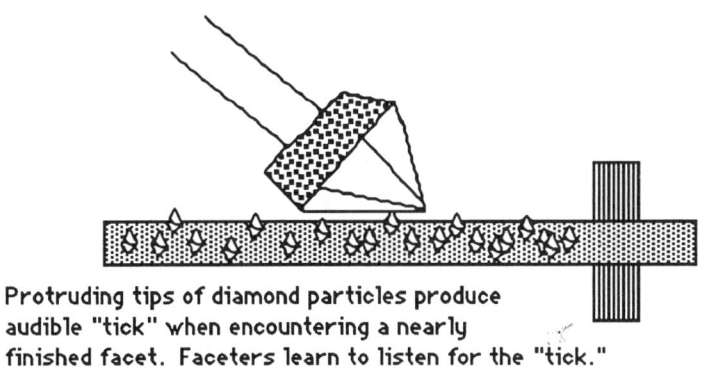

Protruding tips of diamond particles produce audible "tick" when encountering a nearly finished facet. Faceters learn to listen for the "tick."

When a finished facet passes over a diamond lap it will nick random diamond particle tips in the lap surface, producing an audible "tick" sound. This noise will signal that you have reached the stop point.

Faceting With "Ticks" . . .

Learn to facet by the "tick" sound—and you're on the way to becoming a master gemcutter.

What's the "tick" sound?

Well, it's the way most truly capable faceters work. You cut a facet—and listen until all you hear are intermittent ticks, the sound made when the facet trips over random diamond tips on the lap's surface.

When you hear the ticking, you have cut to the stop. You stop cutting that facet and go on to the next one.

On fine laps, though, you can't hear a tick?

Well, that's true if you're cutting on standard laps. You can hear them easily enough on a channel type lap, though. And you should use channel laps. They scratch less, the swarf and debris spins away—and you can hear

Master Gemcutting Tips

the tick.

Some faceters use only channel laps, the type manufactured by Crystalite in Marina del Rey, CA.

You should keep a few standard flat laps at 1500 grit for prepolishing. On a large table facet you want an excellent pre-polish or you'll have all kinds of problems polishing. If you don't use the Crystalite go to one of the Dyna Resin Bonded Laps for pre-polishing use.

Tips in Corundum Polishing . . .

How do you polish corundum?

That's a question asked by many gemcutters.

If you want a good, brilliant polish with a minimum of difficulty, just go to cast iron laps for polish using 14,000 diamond paste. Cast iron with 50,000 diamond grit will

For best polishing corundum and equally hard stones, use a cast iron lap charged with either 14,000 (fast polish) or 50,000 (slower) diamond paste. A Crystalite Last Lap is also effective, especially for smaller stones.

Master Gemcutting Tips

also polish corundum in a hurry, as long as you've given the stone a good 1200 pre-polish.

Be a bit cautious, though: a cast iron lap with even fine 50,000 will do some cutting, too.

You can also use a Crystalite Last Lap with 14,000 for corundum. This combination works well because the metal pelletized resin surface offers the level of hardness that's needed to get the corundum to take a polish.

As usual with any gemstone, pre-polish is the key. Pre-polish on corundum at 1200 and this will suffice. Some faceters urge 3000 pre-polish but it sometimes won't pre-polish because you often get on the basal cleavage. With corundum when you try to pre-polish against the C axis the direction is so hard it won't cut, it will polish.

Plus, a 3000 disc will wear out too quickly running against something as hard as corundum.

When polishing a small corundum consider using 50,000 diamond on a Last Lap, after a 1200 prepolish. For bigger stones, go right to the cast iron lap...that's the real corundum polishing workhorse.

How about spinel or chrysoberyl?

Same way as corundum...cast iron with either 14,000 (for rapid polish) or 50,000 (for a bit slower polish or for smaller stones).

Master Gemcutting Tips

"Running the Wheel"
An Important Cab Technique . . .

Controversial statement or not, most cab cutters simply don't utilize a horizontal grinding wheel to its best advantage.

For years, cabochon instructors have taught pupils to rely on a wiping—and often a rocking— motion for cutting cabochons. This motion dominates cutting practices for ovals and similarly rounded top cabochons.

As a result of these limited cabochon techniques, passed on from one generation of cutters to the next, only a small segment of a cutting wheel is ever used. This obcession holds true for diamond as well as for carbon carbide wheels.

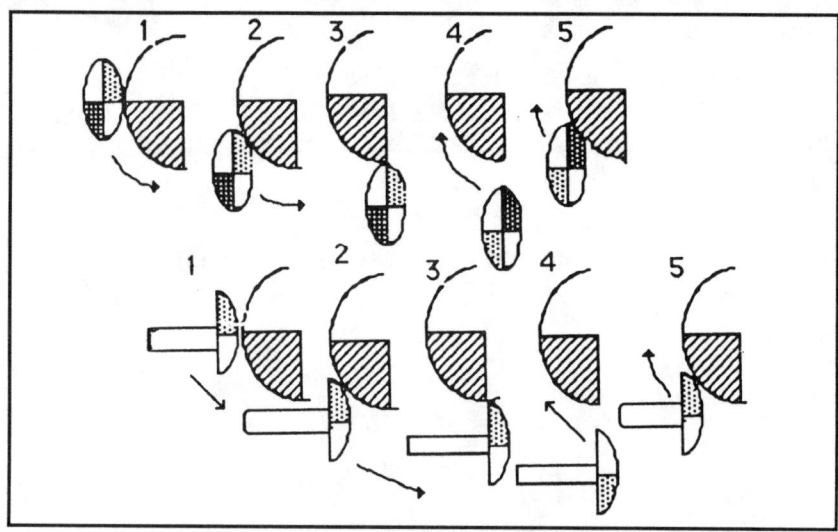

The key to "running a wheel" is to utilize a full quadrant of the wheel's curvature to assist in the cutting. Highly disciplined shapes and curves can be achieved with this method.

Master Gemcutting Tips

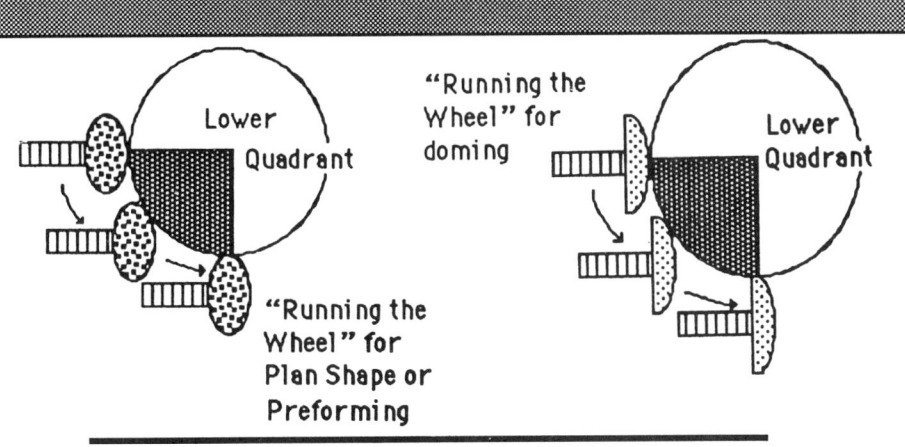

Notice that the dopstick is held strictly horizontal through the running strokes. This enables you to cut shapes and slopes with equal use.

Such traditional methods follow two patterns. A cab cutter holds the cab to the turning wheel with a straight-in orientation and then makes small vertical passes at the wheel, turning the stone slightly with each small swipe. Eventually, the stone is turned through 360° enough times that the beginning of a slope starts to become evident.

The shortcoming in this approach is that each small swipe will be slightly different from the others. As a result, slope control is extremely difficult to maintain and the cabber must go back over the work smoothing down until the apex is properly centered and the slopes even.

Sometimes, hand control and estimating being what they are, a fully disciplined cab can't be accomplished before the cabber runs out of material. One of the critical sight evaluations made of a cabochon is to view it at eye level from the side and rotate the cab in a flat plane so as to survey the slope or curvature profile. Are the slopes smooth and even all the way around the stone? Is the apex centrally located? Are the slopes on the long axis

Master Gemcutting Tips

slightly more shallow than the slopes on the short axis? Is there any indication of under or over cutting in the slopes? Has the cabber left any flats? Does the slope arrive at the girdle line evenly all the way around the stone? Is the girdle line strictly parallel to the base or bottom of the cab? Are the slopes consistently cut?

An expert cabber can very quickly and accurately make a proper assessment as to the quality and discipline of the cutting with this simple visual check. Indeed, one doesn't even need to be an expert to detect a variation in the slope

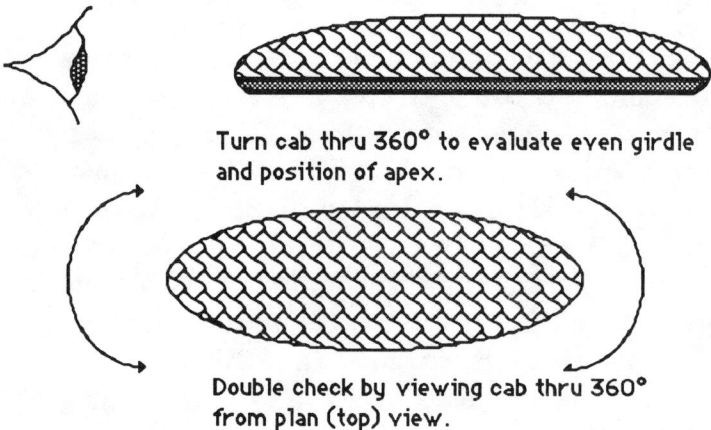

Turn cab thru 360° to evaluate even girdle and position of apex.

Double check by viewing cab thru 360° from plan (top) view.

lines and take corrective actions immediately.

This problem of slope consistency and discipline becomes especially critical when cabbing a star stone or a moonstone. In these cabs you absolutely want a high dome plus an accurately placed apex. In the absence of either, the cutter hasn't released the maximum optical performance of the material. In short, he or she has failed to cut a "good" cabochon...and the reason can usual-

Master Gemcutting Tips

ly be traced to the technique used at the grinding wheel.

In order to correct the shortcomings of the short vertical stroke, many cabbers have turned to "spiraling in" the cabochon crown. This technique consists of separately cutting three rows (usually it's three rows) at a specific declining angle to establish the domed configuration.

The rows are cut about 15-20 degrees apart as shown in the illustration on the previous page. A row can be accomplished by holding the stone in one place on the wheel and turning the dopstick in your hand through 180°.

The only variation in hand control and positioning arises from the difference between the long and short axis of the cab. Round cabochons obviously won't present such a difficulty. Even with oval or steep crowned cabs the varying of pressure to accommodate axis difference is not a particularly difficult problem to overcome.

Once all of the concentric rows—usually cut at approximately 55-35-10 degrees—have been completed the remaining work consists of removing ridges and finishing the apex.

Even then there is always the danger of overcutting. The ridges remove swiftly enough but good pressure control is still needed to finish up with a smoothly contoured slope all the way around the shape. Regardless of the care taken with the concentric rings there remains a need to "clean up" the cutting. Carelessness at this juncture produces the plague of cabochon cutting: flats or unevenesss in shape.

"Run the Wheel"...

Is there a better way of controlling the slope cutting

Master Gemcutting Tips

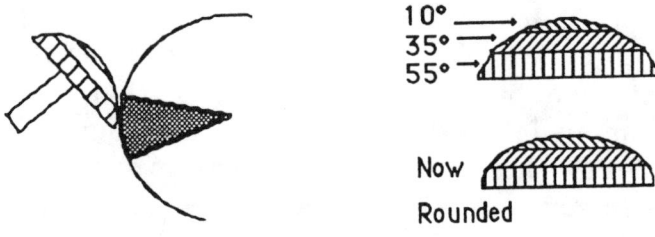

A traditional approach to doming a cab is to cut concentric rings, using a spiraling technique.

demands in cabochon cutting?

Yes, there is a much better way and it's used consistently by the better professional cabochon cutters. The technique is known as "Running the Wheel."

It's not a difficult method to describe or demonstrate. Nor is it too difficult to learn. It works with equal efficiency in preforming a round or oval shape or in cutting the rounded dome. It makes for a remarkable improvement in your cutting speed and shaping discipline.

Briefly, "...running the wheel..." consists of addressing the cabochon flat at the quadrant line of the wheel and keeping the dopstick absolutely straight—as you move toward the bottom of the wheel circle...an arc maximum of 90 degrees. The "Running Stroke" begins with the cab's apex area (if cutting the dome) or the short axis (if shap-

Master Gemcutting Tips

ing an outline) addressed to the stone. Once you've reached the down limit of your stroke, lift the stone away from the wheel momentarily. Then immediately make a complete 180° reverse of the Running Stroke you just performed, this time moving from the bottom of the grinding wheel—with the dopstick still straight to the wheel—and finishing up at the original starting point. You must finish at the same position you started so that the same surface of the stone has twice been exposed to cutting action. "Down, lift, turn 180°, and back..." That's the "Running Stroke" sequence.

There's no more to it than that. It's not really as simplified as it sounds, though. The secret is in learning to

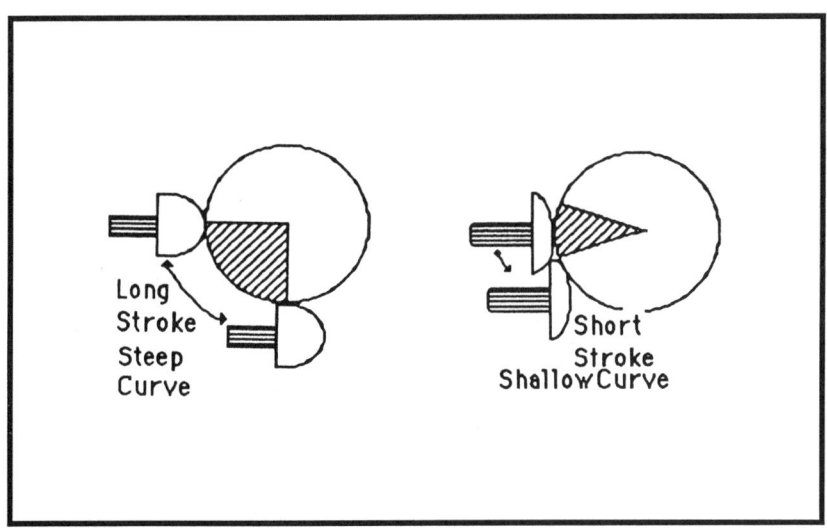

When you "run the wheel" you are using the curvature of the wheel itself to discipline—and make easier—the cutting and shaping operations. It takes a bit of practice, but ultimately provides better shape control and speed.

Master Gemcutting Tips

maintain the appropriate pressure for the rounding or shaping you seek to accomplish—and keeping the dopstick perfectly straight during each stroke. One essential technique produces the best results. That is: after each "Running Stroke" on the wheel, turn the dopstick e.g., the stone completely around 180° and returning the stroke. This simple step tends to even up your cutting and helps produce disciplined slopes...and an apex that is directly in the middle of the cut. What's happening is you can see the cutting results so much quicker.

Also, the distance you run the stone down the turning wheel—and the pressure applied, of course—determines the steepness of the slope.

If you wish to cut a very shallow slope, then use only a short segment of the wheel before you lift off and return. For high domed cabs, make the stroke run from the front of the grinding wheel all the way down to the bottom 90 degrees away, letting up lightly on the pressure as you near the end of the down and the up stroke.

The key to successful Running Strokes is a smooth movement on your part. Don't address the wheel in a herky jerky manner. Place the stone against the wheel and make one, disciplined and continuous movement down the wheel against the turning direction of the wheel itself. Lift off, turn the stone 180°, then reverse the stroke using the same pressure and timing.

It may take a bit of practice to get your strokes down with rhythm and confidence but you'll be astonished at how quickly you pick up the method. Practice a bit on doming a cabochon with a piece of throw away material. Once you have the doming movement down pat try cut-

Master Gemcutting Tips

ting the oval outline shape.

With Running Strokes you'll find that you can cut an almost perfect oval shape without reference to a template. You'll only need a measuring gauge. Eight-inch wheels are preferable for running strokes. Remember: after each down-up stroke, reverse the stone 180° and repeat. This trains your hands to produce a uniform rounding or sloping. That's what you should seek... uniformity in your cutting.

Once you start using a Running the Wheel technique it will become second nature. You're now making the wheel do most of the shaping work because you utilize the curvature of the wheel. Short strokes just don't provide discipline practice because the work on such a small segment produces very shallow curves and doesn't give you a chance to "learn yourself." Pressure and movement control is tough.

The key to successful lapidary is getting to know your equipment—and yourself. When you exert the same control and pressure in every aspect of your cutting you're on your way to true maturation as a gemcutter.

Using Syringes For Fast Epoxy . . .

Many gemcutters have turned away from wax as a dopping agent in favor of fast acting 2-part epoxies.

One gemcutter who has made a successful transition is Doric Ball of Puyallup, WA. He uses Atlas's epoxy "Fast Glue" with a Hardener which sets in five minutes or less.

What makes this epoxy so attractive is the fact that from the time it's mixed it remains a thick paste. Using a

Master Gemcutting Tips

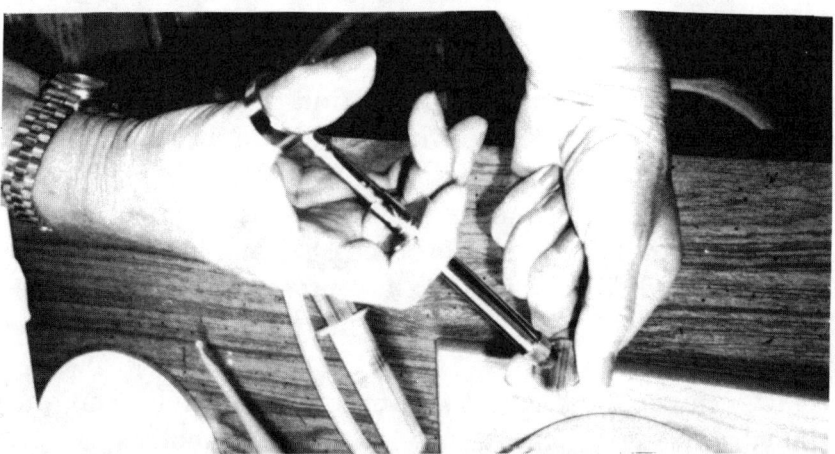

The "messy" accusation leveled so often at 2-part epoxies is removed with a pair of syringes which dispense resin and hardener separately and conveniently. Furthermore, the syringes are reusable.

pair of 3cc syringes with 1-1/2" 21-gauge needles he obtained from a pharmacy, Doric cuts off the needle tips to inch stubs.

He crimps the stubs to create an air tight seal for the syringe. The plunger is then removed and each syringe filled, one with epoxy and the other with hardener. For use, he removes the crimped needle and depresses the plunger. Doric buys the Atlas white "Fast Glue" at a cost of a couple of dollars when ordering the minimum of 6. Order from:

Atlas Minerals
PO Box 38
Mertztown, PA 19539   *1-215-682-7171*

The advantage of placing the components of a two-part epoxy in separate syringes lies in the reusability of the syringes. Unlike the single two-part plunger syringe that

Master Gemcutting Tips

often comes with commercial epoxy, you can refill your own syringes as soon as the supply is exhausted.

Cut Table First, Then Relax & Cut . . .

Here's a tip to remove the worry of polishing a table facet. Always finish the table facet as your first step.

Orient the stone first then hand lap the table flat and pre-polish the table (once the stone gets a tiny flat it will lie still on a turning lap with no difficulty).

The fastest, most effective polishing approach is to drop a Pellon lap over the pre-polish lap, wet it with colloidal silica, and hand polish in seconds a marvelous polish on the flat facet. No facet edge rounding is involved because you're working only with a single, table facet.

Now that you have your biggest polishing problem already solved, dop to the table (sometimes using masking tape between the polished table and the dopstick) and go ahead with cutting the the pavilion. Using an open transfer, remove the stone, dop to the culet and finish the crown facets.

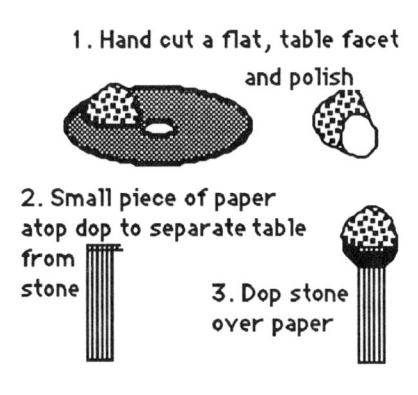

1. Hand cut a flat, table facet and polish

2. Small piece of paper atop dop to separate table from stone

3. Dop stone over paper

After you've finished the star facets the stone is completed—and you'll never have

Master Gemcutting Tips

to face such vexatious tasks as polishing a large table, nipping off star facet tips, "walking the table" across a polish, etc., etc. You merely need to clean the stone: it's done.

Use Baby Shampoo With Diamond . . .

You can save plenty of money by buying diamond dust for your lapidary projects. Yes, the paste is handy but you pay extra for the syringe and the convenience of having a water soluble carrier.

E. W. Zukauchas of Lubbock, TX, has been doing some experimenting with the use of various liquids as a carrier for diamond powder. He finds that Johnson's Baby Shampoo is a marvelous carrier that assures good diamond particle distribution—and is easy and quick to apply to a wheel or lap. Ed warns against liquid soap. For some reason it just doesn't work as well as the Johnson's brand shampoo.

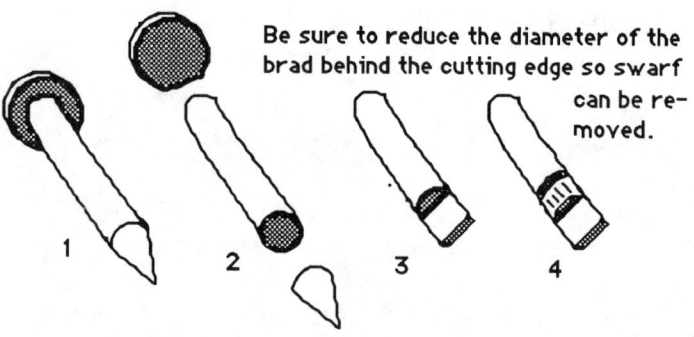

Be sure to reduce the diameter of the brad behind the cutting edge so swarf can be removed.

In making your own tiny drilling tool be sure to reduce the diameter of the brad behind the cutting tip so swarf and cuttings will have exit spacing.

Master Gemcutting Tips

To make certain that the diamond powder is not clumped up when it's introduced to the shampoo, the Texas cutter suggests using a good clean agate mortar and pestle when preparing concentrate for his spray bottles. He uses spray bottles saved from previous purchases to hold his diamond-shampoo mixture.

Drilling Small Holes in Gemstones . . .

Drilling small holes in gems for beading purposes or for stringing in a delicate chain can be particularly troublesome for many gemcutters.

In the absence of tiny enough diamond drills, try using an ordinary brad, a 1x17 (that's one inch long of No. 17 wire). Using a fine grained wheel, grind the head of the brad to the size of the hole you want.

For approximately a quarter-inch behind the head, reduce the body of the brad slightly smaller. You need this smaller diameter directly behind the head so the swarf that's created during the grinding will have clearance to move away from the grinding area. Otherwise, the deeper you drill the greater will be the possibility of splitting the stone.

Use diamond grit and a bit of oil coolant. It should drill out very quickly.

Special Dopstick For Ring Repairs . . .

Many cabbers and faceters are occasionally called upon to repair stones which for various reasons must re-

Master Gemcutting Tips

main in the mounting.

When faced with such a task, orienting the stone to a vertical or horizontal abrasive wheel is not the easiest challenge to perform accurately. For one thing, just holding a ring to a cutting wheel at the proper index and angle is no mean accomplishment.

There is a home-made dopstick that will make this job a lot easier. It consists merely of cutting a diagonal slice or slot across the dopstick about 5/16" from the tip of the stick. This slot serves to hold the bottom of a ring shank. This way the ring can be mounted on the dopstick parallel to the stick's longitudinal axis.

At the tip, drill a hole about 1" deep. Make the hole's diameter slightly larger than the threaded end of a full threaded metal or plastic cap screw. Screw a nut on the threaded section.

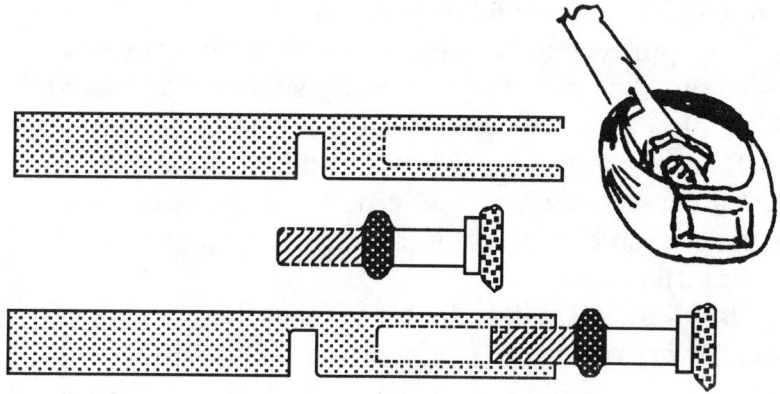

On the cap end, glue or epoxy a layer or two of leather in order to make a soft pad. This soft pad ultimately will be forced against the back of the ring so you want all

Master Gemcutting Tips

hard bolt edges covered lest you may damage the stone or the delicate back of the ring.

That's all the preparations necessary. To use, you slip the bottom of the shank into the dopstick slot. Push the padded end of the cap screw firmly against the back of the ring. Now turn down the nut until it seats firmly against the tip of the dopstick.

The opposing pressure of the padded tip against the back of the ring plus the ring shank slot will present the stone in straight orientation with the end of the dopstick.

With the stone end of the ring now held firmly by the dopstick you can hold the dopstick easily in your hand or in a faceting head quill.

Such a device makes it much easier—and safer—to repair or recut stones without removing them from the mounting.

Cutter Prepares Release Form . . .

Repairing gems can be a very lucrative business for gemcutters. If breakage, though, isn't carefully handled it can be a very disastrous business.

Philip Thompson of Springfield, MA, has an effective release form that he asks his clients to sign before Phil will accept a stone for repair. The wording on his release goes like this:

"In leaving your stone with us for whatever repair is agreed upon, you understand, accept, and fully agree to the following conditions...

"While in our possession, we will take all necessary precautions, and handle your gem in a professional manner at all times, to insure it's safety...

"However, in any gemstone, there may be inclusions,

Master Gemcutting Tips

bubbles, fissures, cracks, and invisible pressures, which the heat and shock of cutting and polishing can cause to develop to the point where the stone can pit, chip, crack, fracture, split, and even explode into several pieces and in some cases, can cause a color change...

"While this rarely happens, should anything of this nature occur, we can not take any responsibility for any damage or loss of value to the stone whatsoever..."

Signature _____ *Date* _____

Effective Method To Remove CA . . .

One of the reasons many gemcutters shy away from the use of epoxies or superglues as a dopping adhesive is this: it's just too darned hard to remove.

Harry Roemmele of Green Bay, WI, seldom has any trouble. And his method for breaking down an epoxy or cyanoacrylate bond is simplicity itself.

Harry simply heats a razor blade and scrapes off some of the hardened adhesive. He holds the dopstick over the flame for a bit to further damage the adhesive. Using a cloth, he then attempts—softly— to tug a little on the stone to see if it will release.

He keeps moving back and forth be-

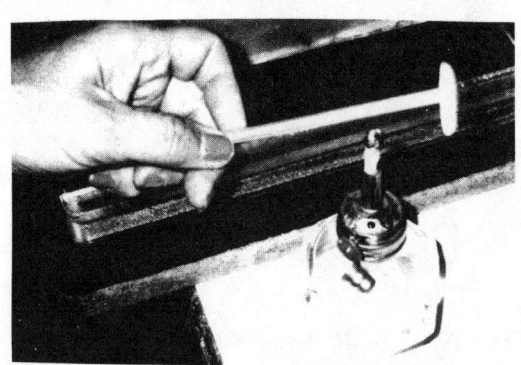

Heat will quickly break down both super glue and epoxies.

Master Gemcutting Tips

tween soft tugs and heat treatment with the lamp flame. Epoxy and cyanoacrylate positively hate heat and eventually will break down. There's no doubt about that.

[Editor's Note: A good technique to inprove safety when removing epoxy and CA with the heat treatment, is to soak a piece of tissue in cold water and wrap the stone with it.

The wetted tissue keeps the stone cool while heating the dopstick destroys the glue.]

Marking Girdles . . .

Another good tip concerns polishing girdles on faceted stones.

When you complete grinding the girdle go ahead and cut the whole half of the stone. On the return re-set for polishing the girdle at 91-1/2°. This will polish only part of the girdle but that's OK: the rest will be cut away when you finish the other half of the stone anyway.

To assure flat-to-flat conditions between the facet and the lap, set up a facet on the correct index

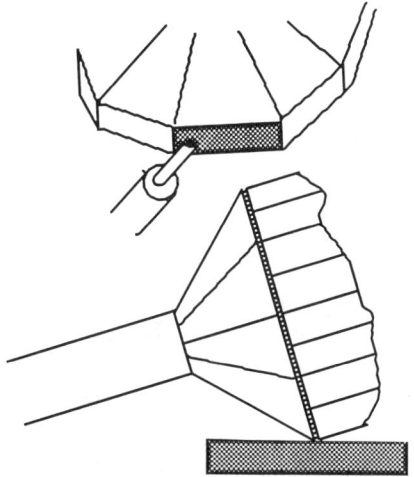

After cutting the girdle facets at 90°, paint them and then set the quill at 91.5° so you'll polish only a thin slice of each girdle facet.

Master Gemcutting Tips

number and then release the trigger while you snap the facet flat.

When you tighten up the index wheel again, you've got the facet flat on the lap.

Avoiding a Shower When Girdling . . .

When girdling a stone, the potential for a free splash shower looms great.

Not only does the faceter open a "gate" in the splash pan, but usually the water flow from the drip tank is set at maximum. The unhappy result of this combination is a steady stream of water and swarf exiting the open area around the dopstick and quill.

The result? A free and uninvited shower of debris spraying the machine and the operator. The girdle may turn out fine, but a major cleanup is usually in order.

Joe C. Smith of Raleigh, NC, has the answer to this difficulty. To control spray he simply uses a wide piece of lamp wick and a paper clip. With the paper clip, Joe fastens the wick onto the bowl edge so that the flat end of the

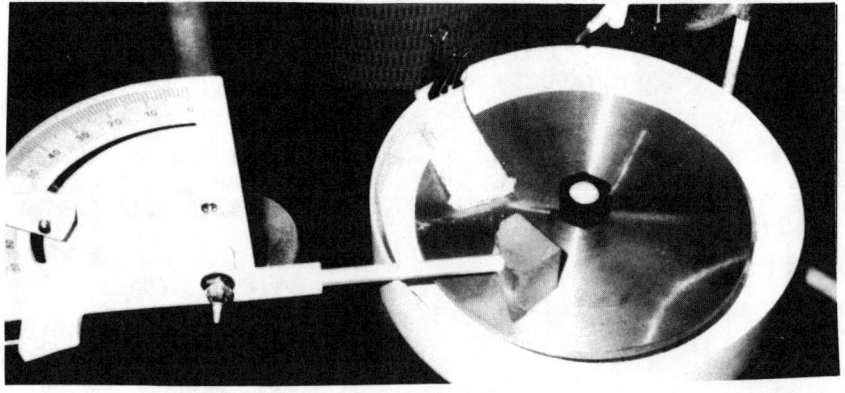

Master Gemcutting Tips

wick rides on the outer edge of his grinding lap.

What happens is quite effective. When Joe turns on the water drip to maximum, the wick simply catches all the splash, smooths it down nicely on the lap and serves as a controlled coffer dam for excess water. Consequently, there is plenty of water coming through the wick to wet and cool the working area—but the free shower is ended. Very little water is available for splashing through the open gate.

When he's finished girdling, Joe removes the wick and slides the gate cover back in place. His machine—and his clothing—are none the worse for wetness.

Star Sapphire Height is Optional . . .

Must a star sapphire be cut higher than half a sphere in order to get the best presentation of the rays?

The answer, from most sapphire cutters, is a resounding, "no." Most star sapphire buyers do indeed like the way the rays spill off a steep apex. For this reason, most star sapphires are cut rather steeply.

But a half sphere will also produce a very attractive star effect. Furthermore, in the mounting of a half-sphere star sapphire cut the setter doesn't have to contend with an inordinately high stone. It's easier setting.

Interpreting Imperfections . . .

Properly interpreting the imperfections of a polished gemstone is vital. Here are the four major imperfection categories:

Master Gemcutting Tips

Good lighting and a magnifier are very helpful in detecting and interpreting various scratches. Orientation of the stone often has something to do with rate of occurrence of scratches and surface conditions.

1. POCK MARKS. These are the easiest to identify and prevent, caused by failure to remove enough material during the lap-polishing operation. They are actually remains of the scratches that were left by the cutting laps.

To manage, just use a finer cutting lap (3000 or 1200) and these will produce the smaller scratches that are easiest to polish out. Pock marks can easily be seen with a 5- or 10-power magnifier.

2. SCRATCHES. Can be seen easily with a conventional Optivisor. Often quite deep and will need considerable polishing to remove (often, polishing simply won't remove them). Scratches aren't always caused by contamination or debris and aggregation. They result mostly from actual burning of rough in a very small area and the resultant cragging of the burned scar across the surface. This occurs because of a concentration of pressure on a tiny spot

Master Gemcutting Tips

which hikes temperature and leads to burning.

You can look in the dark and see scratches as little flashes of light, thanks to irregular reflection. Lap speed is a major factor as some materials will scratch even with very slow rpm and light pressure. Quartz is particularly susceptible to scratching which results from burning. It's best to cut quartz stones at moderate speeds.

Acid or some sort of oxidizer goes a long way to avoid scratching which is due to an accumulation of diamond or chemical powder or swarf hardening. Orientation of the stone with regard to its crystal structure may be a factor. With doubly refractive stones, less scratching is generally experienced when the stone is oriented on the dopstick parallel to the crystallographic axis. Also, some facets just polish faster and easier than others and this same directional hardness phenomena is also observed— some gemcutters claim—in cubic structured crystal forms.

Other Strategies...

Strategies to avoid scratches include changing lap speed, pressure, reversing direction, polishing on a stationary lap, scrubbing a lap with Lava soap or some other strong cleanser, altering the amount and placement of lubrication or chemical powders and, especially, changing the powder-water viscosity. When a polish becomes too dry on the lap it's an open invitation to scratching—yet a too wet polishing environment will cause trouble too. You want it damp-dry.

One final option is to go to a softer lap

3. CAT HAIRS. You'll need 30- to 40-magnification

Master Gemcutting Tips

power to catch these pesky surface imperfections. They are very fine and generally cover a large portion of the facet or surface. Cat hairs often run in the same direction of polish and may be formed during the polishing phase.

The best way to eliminate cat hair problems is to clean the stone surface before polishing and allow a few seconds for any lubricants to "mature" or evaporate. Once found, cat's hairs are easy enough to remove: gently rub the facet or surface back and forth on a stationary lap while changing the angle of the surface to the lap slightly. This latter technique is referred to as "chasing cat hairs" off the lap.

4. PEBBLE FINISH. This kind of surface imperfection occurs very infrequently and is extremely difficult to observe, even with the required 40-diopter. Without strong magnification, you only know you have a pebble finish by the generally unsatisfactory performance of the polished surface: somehow it doesn't come alive as it should.

Pebble finish may actually be due to the orientation of the crystal structure itself. It'll pop up in one stone while another identical one—cut and polished in the same manner—has no problem. Use 100,000 or even 200,000 diamond grit to eliminate pebble finish (often found after you've just removed some cat's hairs).

The reason pebble finish is so hard to diagnose is that the scratch is at or less than the wavelength of visual light.

Cliff Jackson's Wax Lap . . .

For faceters wanting their own wax lap here is the procedure that will produce a highly effective polishing

Master Gemcutting Tips

tool.

This procedure appeared some time ago but the information is still timely:

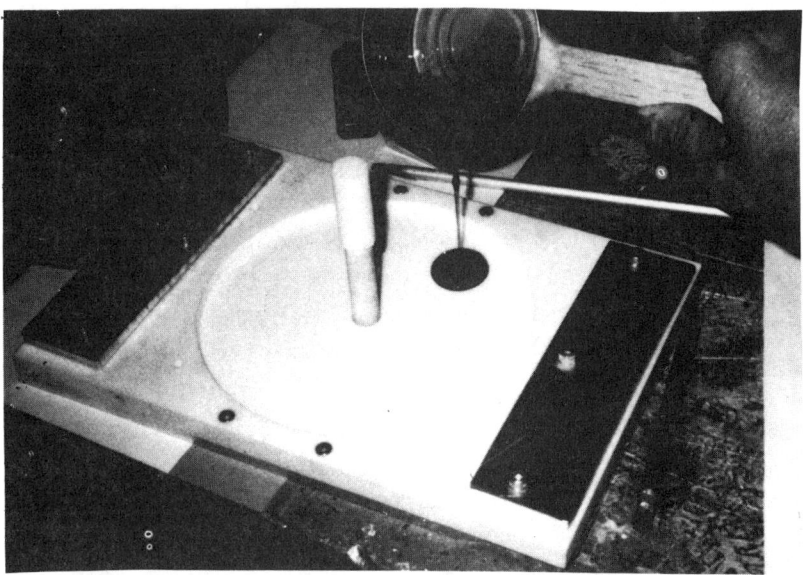

Using Kerr's jewelers master pattern carving wax, medium blue with a small amount of paraffin added, cast the wax nearly 1" thick in disk shapes so laps have substantial strength.

One you've cast the wax into the desired thickness
1. Smooth the surface flat, then score the surface moderately with one wheel of a small knurling tool.
2. With a waterproof laundry marking pencil, make a circle 2 inches from the center for 50,000 diamond grit inside and 8,000 diamond grit on outside rim.
3. Apply the 50M grit by sprinkling the diamond powder over the inside area and adding several drops of light-

Master Gemcutting Tips

er fluid. Rub the diamond into the wax with a rotary motion of the finger. Use the fluid sparingly so you can rub diamond in and feel tackiness as the lighter fluid evaporates. Polish this area with a polishing stone.

4. When you've finished the 50M grit, repeat with the sprinkling and the lighter fluid for 8,000 grit on the outside ring. Be careful because you don't want to contaminate the finer grit area. Use a polished stone to polish.

5. When you've finished rubbing the diamond grit into the wax, polish the ring—working from the inside toward the outside. Polish with a moderately high rpm using water with a heavy concentration of dishwashing detergent. All surfaces of the lap must remain wet with the rpm maintained so any 8,000 particles will spin away and off.

6. For any crystals you intend to polish on your wax lap, first fine grind them with at least 1200 lap. Only when the crystal is properly pre-polished and ALL scratches or imperfections have been removed, should you proceed to the 8000 grit polish and finish up with 50,000.

7. If you experience any scratching, change the lap direction. The laps are good for fluorite, barite, cerussite, sphalerite, calcite, amber and sunstone.

How to Make a Polariscope . . .

Making your own polariscope isn't that tough. You can make one out of two ordinary hair combs.

Simply stand the two combs up on end and glue them into a wood block.

Once the glue has set up, you can then use the comb's

Master Gemcutting Tips

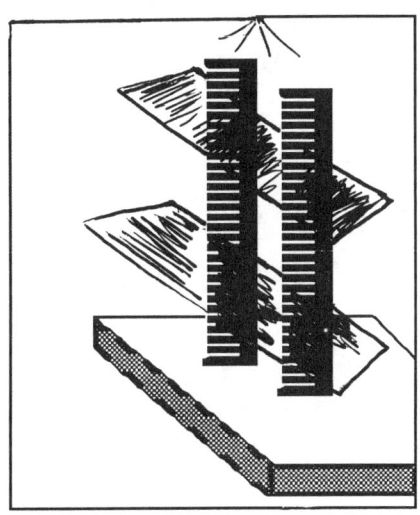

teeth as "holders" and slip the two pieces of polarized film into the teeth. For a light source, thread a small clear Christmas tree bulb through the bottom of the polariscope and now you can find the crystallographic axis with the best of them. Total cost of your homemade polariscope: $2.16.

How do you find the "C" axis of a stone with a polariscope? Turn the polarized film until a view down from the top appears darkest (with the little light on now!).

Turn the stone in a horizonal plane until it blinks four times—light, dark, light, dark—and you're pretty much on the axis. Now twist the stone until the blinking is sharpest ie., the dark and light are strongest and the light changes occurs quickly, abruptly. When you have the stone blinking as sharply as possible, the "C" axis is running from your eye to the light bulb right through the stone.

Thin Polishing Laps Gain Acceptance . . .

More and more gemcutters are following the technology trend of thin polishing laps.

Time was when every faceter solved the bulk of polish-

Master Gemcutting Tips

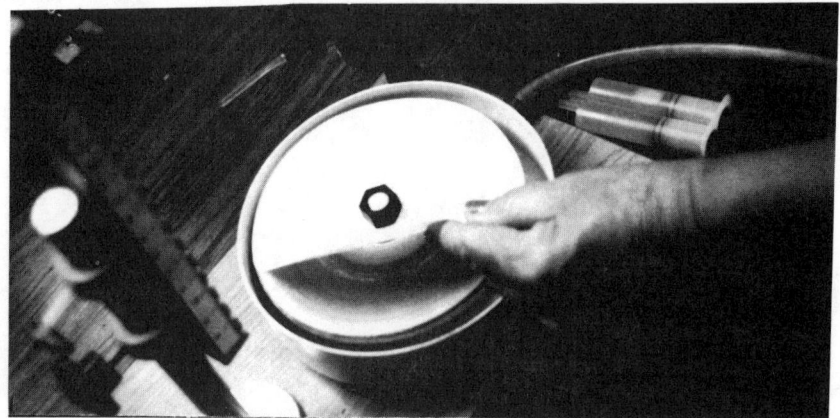

New thin, diamond impregnated polishing laps by 3M and Ultra make it possible to go to polish without removing the pre-polish lap. Just slip on a thin lap, make a slight height adjustment, and go straight to polish.

ing requirements by reaching for some Linde A powder and a tin/lead lap. As a matter of fact, Linde A and the tin/lead lap was introduced by the Graves Company as the best gemstone polishing combination—and Graves still promotes it with good reason.

Still, though, many faceters today are avoiding repeatability and cheating problems by polishing a tier of facets as soon as the tier has been prepolished. With older technologies this usually involved a complete change of laps and then some serious repeatability challenges. With a new polishing lap the dimensions are often slightly different which means the machine setup must be changed so the facet will lay flat-to-flat on the new surface.

As for cabbers, many are also moving away from polishing powders in favor of Bruce Bars and colloidal suspensions. In other words, the powder is just too dirty

Master Gemcutting Tips

to suit their needs—and the paste-like polishing formulations have the additional additives which contribute to faster, superior polishes.

Much of the desire for thicker polishing pastes no doubt has been prompted by the use of diamond grinding and polishing products. Here, various diamond grits are available in a pasty carrier material all nicely packaged in hospital type syringes. Their use is quick, controlled. The diamond pastes can be easily and neatly applied in measured amounts. Further, they can be worked over the polishing surface quite nicely—with control. To save considerable amounts of money, more and more gemcutters are making their own pastes by buying diamond boart loose and mixing it with shampoo, olive oil, and the like.

Still another trend moves toward the permanently impregnated polishing lap. Some samples of this trend are the popular Mirror Diamond Laps, featuring 3M dia-

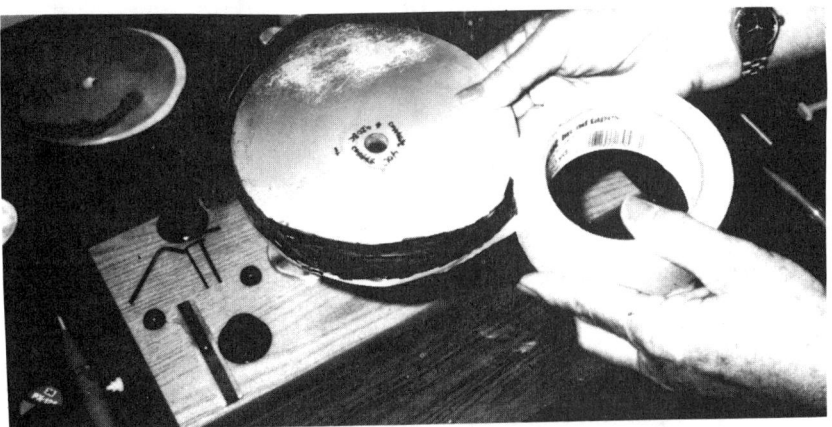

To contain centrifugal sling throwaway of valuable polishing liquids, try building a tape dam or wall around the lap perimeter, or use Ultra laps or Pellon upon which colloidal silica tends to stick.

Master Gemcutting Tips

mond on Mylar, and the Ultra Laps, made by Moyco which feature various oxide polishes impregnated in Mylar.

Colloidal Silica...

Awaiting only a minor technological improvement or two to make it the near universal lapidary polish is colloidal silica.

This remarkable polish was introduced to lapidary by the American Society of Gemcutters of Washington DC, after a series of intensive laboratory examinations at the University of Arizona. A fast acting polish that is especially useful for materials over 7 MOHS hardness, colloidal silica's major drawback is its high viscosity, alkalinity, and affinity for cloth-like polishing pads.

Buehler's Ltd, a major producer of silica along with Crystalite, even sells special polishing pads for use with its silica. The trouble with these perforated pads is that they are almost entirely unsuitable for lapidary. Small facets not only drop through the perforations but the cloth material promotes facet edge rounding. For cabbers, though, the characteristics of the cloth pads are not only acceptable but desirable. The cloth tends to follow the rounding of the cab surface and builds a superior polish.

Still, the disadvantage for both cabbers and faceters is the high viscosity. Fling from the centrifugal action of swiftly turning laps and wheels produces excessive loss of the silica polishing. Gemcutters can only keep supplying polish to the wheel until the supply is exhausted.

In the absence of a thicker, pastier type silica polish, gemcutters are innovating their own responses to the vi-

Master Gemcutting Tips

cosity problem, largely because the polish does such a fine job. These innovations included using colloidal silica on Ultra Laps (for some reason the silica tends to remain a bit longer on the soft chemical impregnated matte finish of the Ultra Lap).

To cut down on fling loss, other gemcutters use masking tape to build a sort of coffer dam on the outer edge of a thick polishing plate. With this paper barrier up, the centrifugal force hurls the silica against the barrier where the gemcutter can swing the stone into the outer edge and work the polish back onto the lap.

The dam idea has been especially popular among gemcutters because colloidal silica actually improves in polishing action after being used a number of times.

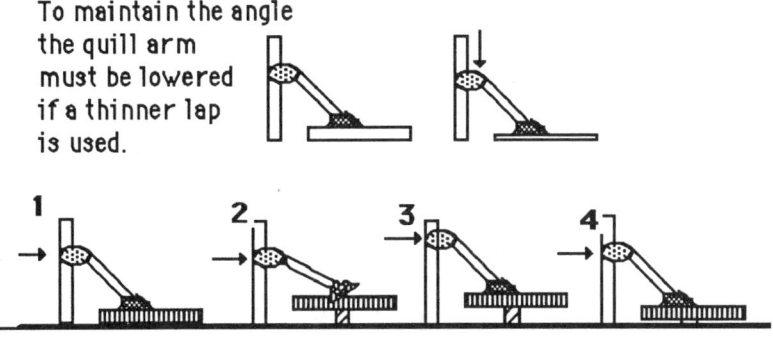

To maintain the angle the quill arm must be lowered if a thinner lap is used.

By using laps of the same thickness, you avoid the need to keep making height adjustments on the mast. Note in **(2)** how the elevation of the lap's surface flattens out the quill arm and forces a change **(3)** to accomodate.

One of the major complications in faceting is the "misalignment" factor that occurs when height settings must be changed to accommodate different thicknesses of laps. Thin vinyl laps remove much of this problem because the adjustment is so minor.

Master Gemcutting Tips

Some gemcutters report they have re-used colloidal silica up to a dozen times. The swarf? It's apparently the material that improves the silica's polishing action.

Mirror Facets...

What has made the Mirror Faceting Kit™ so popular among faceters is the fact that diamond grit has been used to impregnate the thin 3 mil Mylar surface—and consequently they are an easy-to-use product.

The thinness is greatly appreciated by faceters. Once they've prepolished a tier it's a simple matter to wet down the prepolishing lap and drop on a thin Mylar diamond polishing lap. A few up clicks on the vertical cheater is about all that is necessary to adjust for the dia-

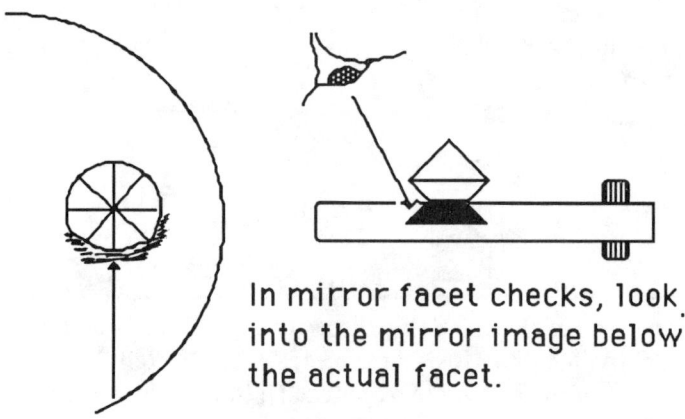

In mirror facet checks, look into the mirror image below the actual facet.

The mirror system makes use of an old machinist's trick for evaluating flat surfaces. Wet the facet, place it on a mirror and then "read" the reflection you see in the mirror underneath the facet.

Master Gemcutting Tips

mond polishing lap's thickness. The faceter is immediately ready to commence polishing. And the whole operation is clean.

The same holds true with Ultra Laps. Moyco reportedly is coming out with its own line of diamond impregnated laps but for now Ultra Laps mean polishing with permanently impregnated tin oxide, chrome oxide, and cerium oxide. Just wet the holding lap and make certain the water flow is swift over the polishing side, too.

Like the Mirror Laps, the Ultra Laps require only a few up clicks on the vertical cheater to accommodate their thickness. Not only are the Ultra Laps clean and convenient, they are also relatively inexpensive. Most rock and gem dealers have them, so availability is also outstanding.

Mirror Facet Kits™ are available from:
Prospector's Pouch, Inc.
Box 112
Kennesaw, GA 30144   1-404-427-6481

The proprietor of Prospector's Pouch, Inc. is J. R. Smith who has developed a remarkably effective faceting system using these thin 3M diamond pads. Not only does the Mirror Facet Kit™ allow a faceter to avoid height changes when changing laps from grinding, sanding, and polishing, but Smith has developed a mirror finished master lap that can be utilized so as to check on the flatness of facets, too.

A complete series of diamond grit laps come with the kit and it is recommended that a beginning or veteran faceter try this effective lap system.

Master Gemcutting Tips

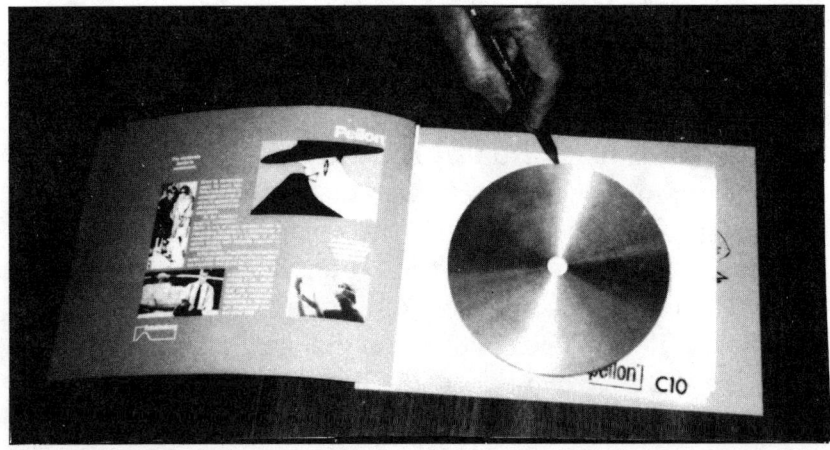

Making a Pellon lap is easy: pencil in a circle of the desired diameter, cut out the disk with scissors, and slip over a master lap.

Thick Acetate . . .

Even with such fine products as the Mirror and Ultra Laps, gemcutters continue to innovate.

Two of the best innovations are the use of Pellon and of Acetate laps. Acetate is used for blue prints and is often available as scrap or throw away from engineering or blue printing shops.

Pellon is a cloth-like plastic material used as a backing material in print shops and tailoring shops. It is also made for linings and serves effectively as a clothing stiffener.

You can use Pellon in a couple of ways. It is very effective for faceting, cabbing, and flat polishing when glued to a stiff backing or a metal disk and then charged with chemical-water mixes. Be on guard against sharp edges or hooks in the stone material: these can catch the Pellon material and rip. Look for Pellon in any yard goods

Master Gemcutting Tips

store. Standard lapidary cement will hold it to a lap.

[Editor's Note: Many gemcutters dispense with gluing Pellon to a master lap. They slip it over a master and then use the arbor nut to keep it in place.]

If you do elect to cement Pellon to a master disk, it's a good idea to iron the material first to remove wrinkle. Apply the cement evenly to avoid bubbles. If you get bubbles, work them out with your fingers toward the edge.

John Sinkankas, noted lapidary author, reports that Pellon Laps are especially efficient for quartz and chalcedony flats. Use cerium oxide and Linde A for best results.

Faceters who have worked with Acetate materials insist that a couple of easy-to-follow rules will produce good results:

First, get the extra heavy Matte Acetate which is about .0065" thick. This is much thicker than Ultra Laps because the Acetate is used in visual arts applications. As a

Feel the acetate with your fingers to identify the textured side: this is the side to use for polishing. Pellon can simply be traced, scissored out, and used.

Master Gemcutting Tips

result, it is much less likely to tear, fold, or rip when exposed to heavy polishing pressures.

Even if the blue print has lettering and writing on it the Acetate material is still usable. It can be removed with soap and water—or by polishing action which will remove it in record time.

Use a standard 6" or 8" lap as a template and outline the round shape and 1/2" arbor hole with a felt tipped pen. A pen writes best, of course, on the side with the textured finish. Use this textured side for polishing.

For polishing use, a thick Acetate lap is used the same way as a Mirror or Ultra Lap. Just make certain you have plenty of water on the base lap to assure good suction ie., adhesion of the polishing lap and master lap.

Here are a couple of tips for applying polish. A paste—whether diamond or chemical oxide—works best. The new colloidal oxide polishes now sold by Magi of Bea-

It's really not all that messy to apply polish with your fingertips. Develop your skill at applying polish this way and you'll save time—and not waste polish.

Master Gemcutting Tips

vercreek, OR, is perfect for this kind of application. In the absence of these permanently suspended polishing pastes, mix up a thick slurry of oxide and water. Once the lap is turning and you have a reasonable water drip flow set up you can apply the oxide-water paste with your finger tips, smearing it on near the spindle and finger pressing the polish out toward the outer edges.

With diamond, try making a two-tone lap. Use a grease pencil while the lap is turning to mark a ring about two inches in from the edge on an 8" lap and one inch in on a 6" lap. Stop the machine and apply a couple squirts of 8000 mesh diamond paste on the line. Drag your finger through the small diamond paste mounds. Smear it around the outer ring.

Use the same procedure with 14,000 or 50,000 mesh diamond paste on the inside near the hub. Make sure your fingers have been cleaned from the previous operation: you certainly don't want contamination problems. Also, remind yourself to wipe off a stone or facet after using it in the 8000 ring before proceeding to the inner 14,000 diamond mesh area.

Bruce Bars come in handy with these thick Acetate polishing pads. You aren't restricted to diamond pastes. Mark the lap with a grease pencil as before and then apply Aluminum Oxide Bruce Bar to the outside ring. The inside polishing area is treated with Linde A Bruce Bar. This combination, incidentally, is dynamite for YAG. Each Acetate polishing lap should be dedicated: a different one for each polish type.

Master Gemcutting Tips

For Brilliance Cut a Sunflower . . .

Hans J. Theiler of Spartanburg, SC, enjoys a truly brilliant cut gemstone.

He's tried all the new De Beers designs and has focused his attention on the Sunflower Cut. Says Hans, "How can you improve on it?"

If you like to enjoy a good challenge and cut a stone that offers sparkle and brilliance try some of the new De Beers designs, including the Sunflower. These cuts were developed by De Beers to promote lightly colored diamonds. The designs, therefore, are excellent for use by colored stone cutters with only slight modifications.

Sunflower

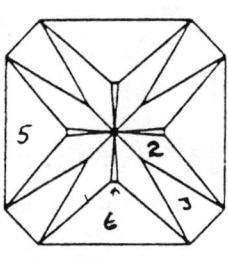
BOTTOM VIEW

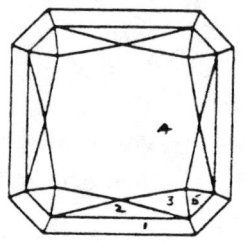
TOP VIEW

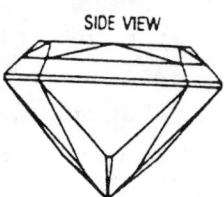
SIDE VIEW

PAVILION

Step	Angle	Index	Comments
1	90	96-24-48-72	Sides
2	41	95-01, 23-25, 47-49, 71-73	Culet
3	41	12-36-60-84	3/5 to Culet
4	90	12-36-60-84	To #3 facets
5	42+	96-24-48-72	3/4 to Culet (This angle varies depending on stone size.)
6	41+	96-24-48-72	meet at culet. Polish in, don't cut

CROWN

Step	Angle	Index	Comments
1	43	96-24-48-72	makes girdle 2-36-60-84
2	35	96-24-48-82	width of #1 half the height of crown
3	27*	94-02, 22-26	Vary to get height of #2 equal to #1
4	0	Any index	Table
5	30*	12-36-60-84	

* approximate

Master Gemcutting Tips

DAHLIA

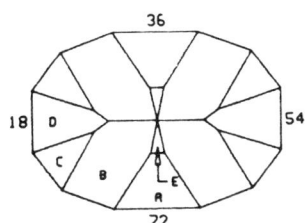
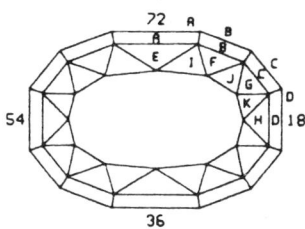
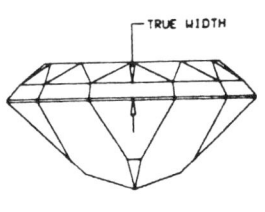

CROWN		
Step	Angle	Index
A	46	72-36
B	46	3-33-39-69
C	46	10-26-46-62
D	46	18-54
E	36	72-36
F	36+	3-33-39-69
G	36+	10-26-46-62
H	36	18-54
I	32+	1-35-37-71
J	31++	6-30-42-66
K	30++	15-21-51-57

PAVILION		
Step	Angle	Index
A	46++	72-36
B	42	3-33-39-69
C	43	10-26-46-62
D	42	18-54
E	42+	72-36

FIRE ROSE ROUND

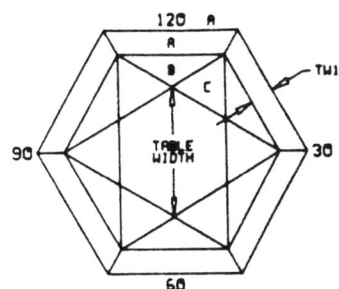
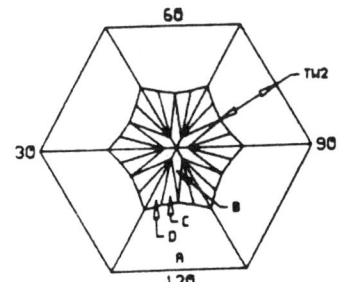

120 Index
Girdle 120-20-40-60-80-100

CROWN
Step Angle Index
A 46 120-20-40-60-80-100

B 36 120-20-40-60-80-100
C 22++ 10-30-50-70-90-110

PAVILION
Step Angle Index
A 52 120-20-40-60-80-100

Master Gemcutting Tips

B 42   120-20-40-60-80-100
C 42+ 1-19-21-39-41-59-
        61-79-81-99-101-119

D 42   2-18-22-38-42-58-62
        78-82-98-102-118118

ZINNIA

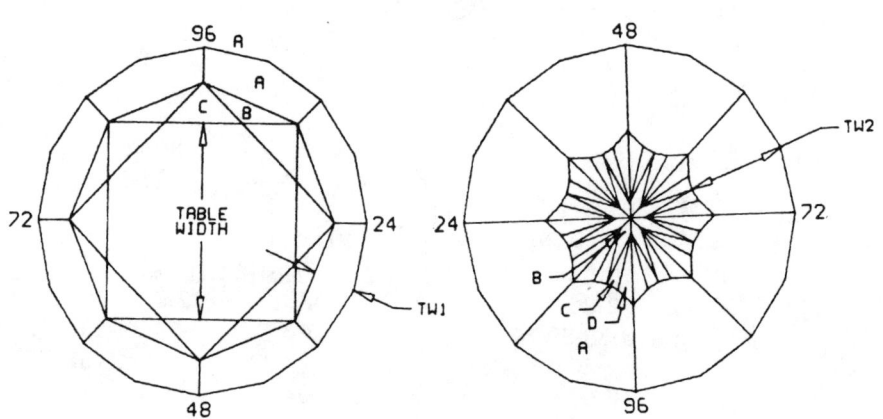

Girdle 96 Index
        3-09-15-21-27-33-39-45
        51-57-63-69-75-81-87-93

CROWN
Step   Angle   Index
A 46   6-18-30-42-54-66-78-90
B 36   6-18-30-42-54-66-78-90
C 21+ 96-12-24-36-48-60-72-84

PAVILION
Step Angle   Index
A 52+ 6-18-30-42-54-66-78-90
B 42   6-18-30-42-54-66-78-90
C 42+ 5-7-17-19-29-31-41-43
        53-55-65-67-77-79-89-91
D 42+ 3-9-15-21-27-33-39-45
        51-57-63-69-75-81-87-93

Note: On these special designs a plus (+) after the angle indicates you should cut slightly past the angle. A double plus (++) indicates you should cut well past the angle, at least more than half way to the angle.

Master Gemcutting Tips

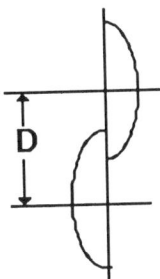

Bill Horton's "Drunken Oval" . . .

Here is a unique approach for developing a cabochon design called the "Drunken Oval."

William "Bill" Horton of Howell, MI, took a top award in the national Pinnacle Awards gemcutting competition for new cabochon designs with this entry.

Here's how Bill suggests you design a Drunken Oval.
1. Draw an "X" and "Y" line.

2. Select an oval template of your choice. Mark one

Master Gemcutting Tips

half of the oval on either side of the "Y" line.

3. Make "D" distance of your choice. It will determine the length of your cabochon.

4. Draw a line from the tip of each oval half to a Tangent of the oval. This will set up the periphery of the cabochon and the width (W)

5. If the width is not enough, draw an additional line to be parallel to the "Y" axis line. Draw the oval again and extend it to the parallel line. This now gives you the proper width for the cabochon.

6. Draw the template on card copy or cardboard, and transfer the drawing to a cabochon flat. **Note:** the tip can be sharp or you can round it slightly.

Proper Lighting is Important . . .

Setting up a properly lighted work area makes a tremendous difference in your finished stones.

Here's a suggestion from Herb Hirata of San Angelo, TX.

Herb uses two lights: 1) a 300-watt Halogen outdoor floodlight ($12 at Wal-Mart) over his right shoulder, 20

Master Gemcutting Tips

inches from the dopstick-up position of the machine, and 2) a clamp-on 3-foot flexible work lamp with a clear 100 watt bulb ($25 at K-Mart).

The clamp-on is used to augment the Halogen light by moving the former around to eliminate any shadows. The Halogen light makes it easy to see the facet edge alignment as well as any dull spots on a facet during polishing.

Improper lighting can compound a recognition problem, Herb warns.

Consistent Polish Requires System . . .

Placing and keeping your polishing slurry on the lap or buff consistently takes a system, says W. R. Ehney of Newberry, SC.

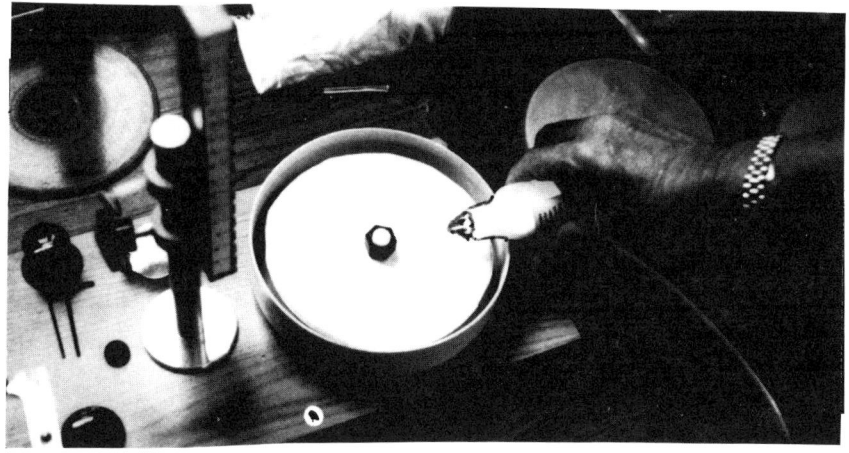

Water control is vital for keeping the necessary damp-dry surface condition on a lap surface. Place some polish near the arbor post, then add a drop or two of water intermittently so the paste will flow, but not lose consistency.

Master Gemcutting Tips

What W. R. does is place a drop of polishing paste near the spindle with the machine on slow speed. He then adds a drop of water at selected intervals so as to maintain the dry-damp state that produces good results.

This action keeps the lap sufficiently wet but centrifugal force still carries the polish to the outer edge of the lap.

W. R. did considerable testing with various colloidal polishing samples provided to him. He found he got excellent results—on a Phenolic lap—along with Linde A, Tin Oxide and Cerium Oxide. Using the same lap, he reports only average success with Chromium Oxide and Colloidal Silica. The latter polish prefers a cloth-like surface.

A Trick For Even Girdles . . .

George W. Seaman of Framingham, MA, was having trouble getting an even girdle on his faceting machine.

Yes, some faceting machines have accessories for cutting precise girdles but George didn't have one. So, he

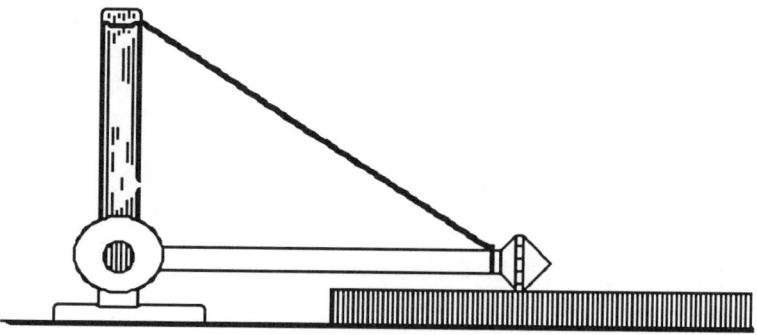

By attaching a non-stretching wax cord to the end of the quill and the top of the mast, precise girdles can be cut on any faceting machine.

Master Gemcutting Tips

placed the stone in the free wheeling position, took a piece of waxed string (the kind used by surveyors) and tied a small loop on one end. He then attached the loop to the tighten retention screw on the spindle.

Turning the index gear, he wrapped the string around the spindle five to 10 times. Now with the machine in the 90° position and a 1200 grit lap adjusted to cut a small amount of material off, he lowered the gem onto the lap with his right hand. While holding a steady pressure and at the same time pulling the string with an even and steady speed, he cuts a perfect girdle every time effortlessly and confidently.

Papier Maché For Unique Jewelry . . .

It's the rare gemcutter who doesn't have a custom cut stone pocketed away somewhere in his or her workbench. That stone will stay there, too, until it's owner finds someone—or self—who'll produce a customized design to acccommodate its unusual shape.

The unfortunate aspect of this gemcutter dilemma is that many have such cuts. But these owners are gemcutters, not goldsmiths. Therefore most custom stones owned by gemcutters will probably never occupy a proud place in a mounting and become part of a jewelry piece. Their fate is to take up space in a drawer or plastic bag— or be given or thrown away.

If you have such cuts, take heart. A simple inexpensive way exists to convert these "space takers" into beautiful jewelry items. You don't need to be a goldsmith either.

The answer lies in a material called papier maché.

Master Gemcutting Tips

This is the same material that school children and avant garde artists use to sculpture. Recently, papier maché has been showing up in fancy boutiques as a new kind of jewelry complete with gemstones and baubles. What these designers are doing is making ear rings and pendants out of the material. Because it has surprisingly good strength, papier maché is even being designed with gemstones and metal findings. A judicious application of paints gives the piece a unique appearance.

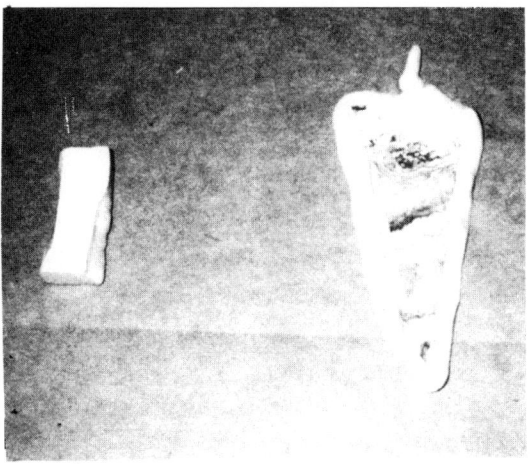
Papier maché is an excellent material for making a fast, easy, inexpensive jewelry item.

Easy to Customize...

What makes a jewelry making experiment with papier maché so attractive for many gemcutters is that they can easily and inexpensively produce custom jewelry pieces. At the same time, with papier maché a cutter can also produce display modules and parts for exhibitions.

Working with maché is not difficult The material is sold mostly at stores or artist\hobby shops. It's simply mixed with water and then molded with the fingers. Drying times vary with temperature and humidity but it's usually less than half-an-hour.

Once a piece is finished, it can be sanded smooth and

Master Gemcutting Tips

painted. Surprisingly smooth finishes can be achieved with a bit of patience—and elbow grease.

Opal Cutting/Polishing . . .

If a universal lapidary stone exists it must be opal. Opal can be faceted, cut en cabochon, carved and sculpted, and even made into jewelry in the rough.

Regardless of the use, it invariably produces awesome optical and color performance. As any experienced gemcutter realizes, opal offers a majestic result but en route it can be fraught with challenges...heat sensitivity, porosity, softness, easily chipped, unpredictability. The list certainly could be made longer—which is probably why many gemcutters like to accept the opal challenge.

Most of the finest material—actually some 90%-95% of

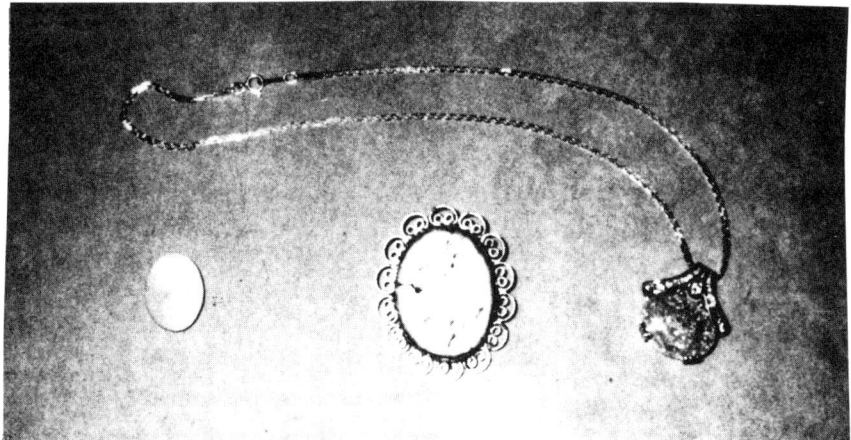

Opal offers optical excitement—plus plenty of challenge in cutting. It's a good idea to shape this soft, colorful stone with at least a 260 grit wheel or higher to avoid cracking or splitting...or cutting through the color layer. Most color develops in thin, variable layers or veins.

Master Gemcutting Tips

the world supply—comes from Australia. Most of this is seam opal mined in Coober Pedy, Andamooka and Mintabie in South Australia, and from White Cliffs and Lightning Ridge in New South Wales. Western Queensland produces the other main type of opal, boulder opal.

As critical as effective opal cutting can be, the first principle is: buy effectively. You can't get water from a stone, warmth from an ice cube, or color from potch. The key to cutting a beautiful, valuable opal is first buying opal that contains the fire. No amount of cutting can covert mediocre opal to beauty.

This is not always easy to do which is why working with opal can be a delightful "crap shoot." It is definitely a

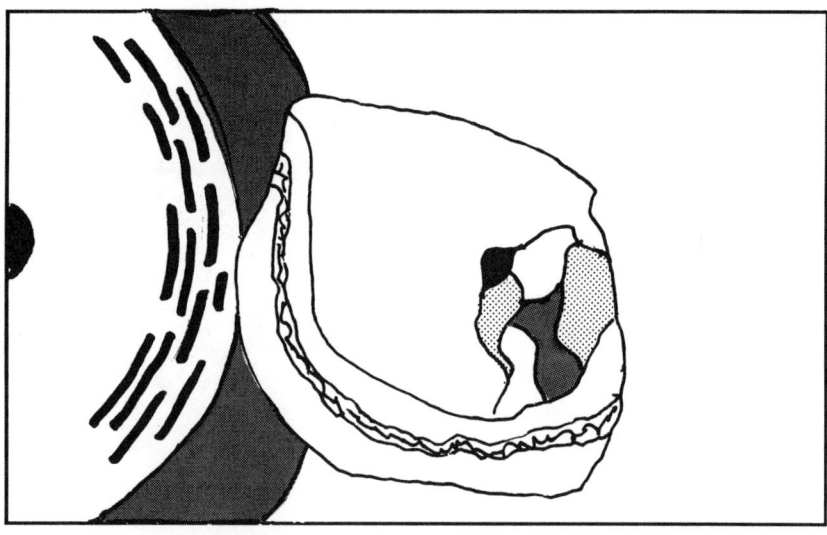

The first step in opal cutting is to locate the band of color by grinding lightly all around the edge of the rough piece. When wetted the stone will usually reveal the color band. If all the potch is not removed, be sure to leave a layer of potch on the side opposite from the viewing side.

Master Gemcutting Tips

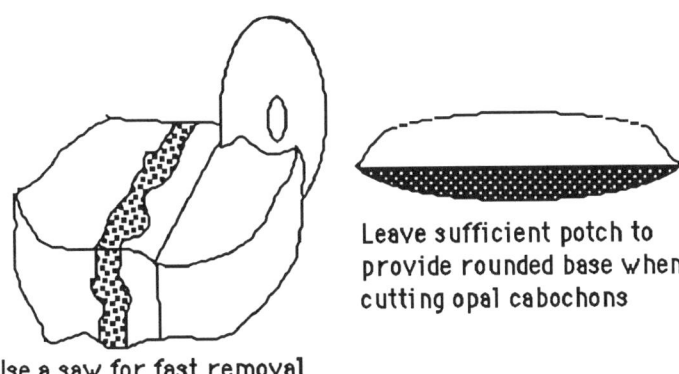

Use a saw for fast removal

Leave sufficient potch to provide rounded base when cutting opal cabochons

Grind a shallow, slightly rounded back (it can always be thickened if desired by attaching a laminate material) and then initially sand with 360 or 400 diamond or carbide paper. Use a magnifier throughout to view.

---

gambler's stone—up to a point.

Buy Carefully...

When you buy opal, subject it to a wet and a dry examination. Your eyes will usually give you most of the clues to the color content and hints as to location. Color will usually reveal itself along the edges of the opal piece—especially when you are inspecting wet opal.

The old fantasy that opal must be kept in water to avoid drying out and crazing is just that, a fantasy. Opal is kept in water only to reveal its color. When checking for cracks and other flaws clean the opal and then inspect it dry. Look for cracks and rusty-colored streaks which usually turn into flaws later. Sand patches and areas of blank potch play havoc on the final size and shape of an opal so pay attention to aberrations in the material.

It's not usually necessary to inspect with a magnifier or loupe. If the color needs magnification to see it, then

Master Gemcutting Tips

you're probably dealing with a low quality specimen. The rule of arm for inspecting opal colors in that the color should be evident when held at arm's length.

Opal Types Cutting ....

Cutting approaches to seam and boulder opal differ markedly. Most opal cutting is performed on seam opal so the discussion here will focus on that type.

There may be only two broad types of opal, but the major one—seam opal—comes in a variety of forms. It can come in very thin bands covered with clay or sandstone, or come in chunks with patches of color mixed in with the potch. Most of the seam opal available to U. S. cutters comes in flattish pieces with a band of precious opal. To more properly evaluate the extent and quality of the color vein, grind gently all around the piece. In most cases, the vein will be on the thin side and your task will be to cut

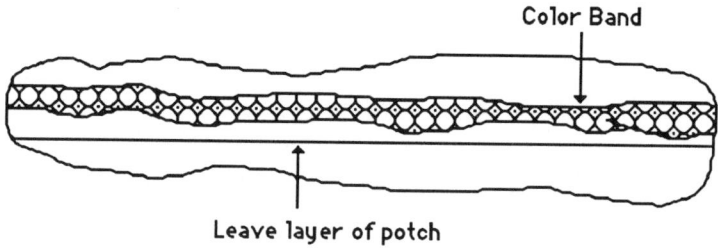

Because color orientation is the most critical step in opal cutting, take time to determine the best angle and cut depth. View with a magnifier for any cloudy potch cover whose removal could mean a brighter stone.

Master Gemcutting Tips

down to the color layer while leaving potch on the underside to lend thickness and strength to the final pitch.

Most opal, of course, is cut to standard shape. It's often a more profitable alternative to allow the stone's color layer to dictate the final shape. More and more gemcutters are following this philosophy of cutting because it allows for bigger, higher quality cut stones.

Inspect With Magnifier...

Before making an arbitrary decision as to which side of the color view to cut down to, use a magnifier and inspect the color vein carefully. Often one side of the vein will produce more showy colors than the others. Even though you can only inspect from the edge of the stone a good magnifier, aided by stone wetness will often reveal the best side.

Once you've made your cutting choice take the opal piece to the saw and remove the blank potch area with saw

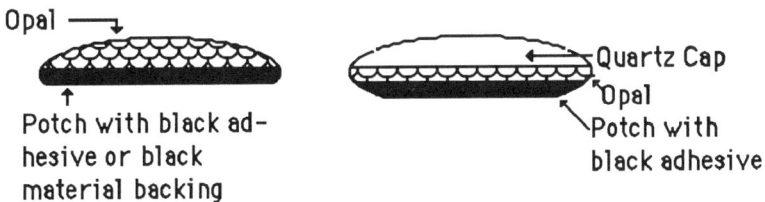

When confronted with a very thin color seam, such as boulder opal, consider shaping only and not polishing or going to a doublet or triplet construction to enhance existing color. In any event, leave some potch on the back.

Master Gemcutting Tips

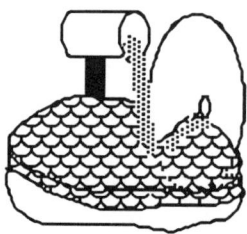 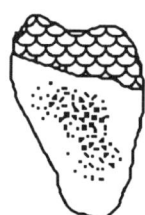

Use plenty of water. If you use oil the liquid will penetrate the crystal lattice and become almost impossible to remove satisfactorily.

When sawing opal try to use only water as coolant. Oil tends to clog up the mineral lattice; it can be very hard to remove later.

cuts. Most professional opal cutters use water only as a coolant, mindful that oils and even soluble oils can penetrate the porous material.

Try to keep a flat surface at a right angle to the direction of the saw cut. Opal isn't all that sensitive but a flat surface upon which to plant the opal piece down to the saw bed is preferable so as to minimize chatter and possible breakage. Opal is soft and cuts easily but its brittleness can indeed be troublesome.

You'll find that a saw cut parallel to the color vein will remove most of the overburden and allow you to get to the color cutting straight away. As for the bottom of the stone, the rule of thumb here is that the thickness below the color layer should be about the thickness of the mounting into which the stone will be placed. If the stone is being cut for speculation, a thickness maximum of 5mm-8mm should suffice.

Master Gemcutting Tips

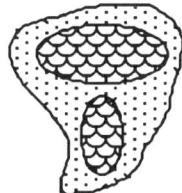 

Consider allowing the opal's natural shape to dictate the final design. Good opal is too expensive to waste. Notice the amount wasted when the gemcutter forced oval shapes into the rough

Opal cabochons in an oval shape are traditional, yes, but remember that opal is an expensive material and shape planning should always involve the economics of cutting. Often, allow rough shape to dictate shape.

Decide on Shape...

The decision on shape is an important one. If you're cutting relatively inexpensive material with significant amounts of potch then cutting to one of the calibrated shapes is a reasonable option.

When the material is quite valuable, though, you'd best allow the color layer to determine the final shape. It's inconceivable that a gemcutter would waste highly valuable color portions merely for the sake of a standard size. Before you can truly make a final decision on the shape you need to know the parameters of the color layer.

Cutters who have worked a great deal with precious opal generally saw cut a fragment down to the fire layer, mindful that the backing potch must also be the right depth. From there, a 400 silicon carbide wheel or belt or a 600 or 1200 diamond wheel can be used to slowly remove

Master Gemcutting Tips

the potch on the top of the stone. Grinding is continued until the fire layer begins to show through.

Once you've got the top part taken off, give the piece a careful look. Can you make a reasonable analysis of the color content? The arm's length test is valuable here. Hold the stone—wet—at arm's length and study the color pattern. Does the color remain continuous over most of the top surface? What's the maximum width and length dimensions that you can realize without a no-color condition?

With respect to color requirements, is the fragment large enough to hold in your hands or should it be dopped? Size and the final configuration will make this decision. If you do decide to dop, make it a cold dop using shellac and then dopwax (NEVER heat the opal directly or quickly) or use a superglue with an accelerator.

Working on the cutting surface and edges of a silicon carbide or diamond wheel, cut the plan view so that it involves color right up to the edges. Cut a few opals and you'll get the hang of cutting a shape to maximize color.

After this preliminary step is finished, direct your attention to the bottom of the stone. Some cutters dome the bottom (to increase the weight for "per carat" sales) but much opal cutting is oriented toward a flat back with a distinct girdle line to accommodate prongs. More and more opals are now coming through with a modest dome on the bottom.

This dome isn't necessarily for weight as it is for added strength. A domed back is also quicker and easier to do. When the preliminary grinding has been completed, move to a belt sander or rubber backed disk grinder of 600

Master Gemcutting Tips

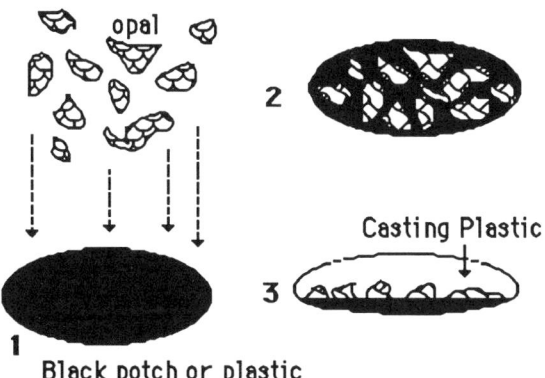

Never throw away cutting fragments if they contain color. Later, these fragments can be placed in a cab or custom shape, covered with polyester clear plastic and made into a marvelous and colorful creation.

---

grit. This makes it easier to obtain the soft rounding that is so becoming in an opal. Also, new research and findings on fractures induced by coarse grit makes it advisable to work an opal with 600 grit or finer.

Incidentally, many opal cutters prefer to work with a dopstick regardless of the size of the stone. They explain that it's easier to manipulate the stone against a sanding belt or pad with a dopstick, especially when working on a rounded bottom or top.

After the 600 grinding, go to a 1200 pad—either silicon carbide or diamond—for the pre-polishing. Don't forget to do the domed back carefully. This can be sanded with 1200 only or taken all the way to high polish if you wish. When you've completed the back you're now ready to attend to the top. Re-dop if necessary. If you've put in a domed bottom, you'll surely need an accelerator with superglue in

Master Gemcutting Tips

order to get the "fill" necessary to form a bond between the dopstick end and the curved opal surface. Also, allow the attachment to sit a bit longer before working. This will give the cyanoacrylate more time to set up.

Color Angles Vary...

It goes without saying that the color location on a section of opal is rather unpredictable. Faced with a chunk of potch which shows no exterior color and allows no clues, some cutters suspect that the best color presentation will be perpendicular to the thickness of the stone.

This is not always the case. The disciplined color display can be at almost any angle to the shape of the stone. Only by wetting (this gives almost the appearance of a polished surface) and turning a section of rough to and fro under the light can you properly assess the best way to cut the stone and enhance its maximum color potential. Sometimes an opal's color is camouflaged by a cloud film that covers the color layer. When you encounter such a condition study the film carefully under magnification. This film will reduce the color brilliance and it's wise to grind down a bit more to see if the film can be removed and greater color potential released.

Often the cloudy film will continue throughout the color layer and you must use your own judgement where to discontinue any additional removal. Experience is the best teacher here.

Careful analysis is vital when it comes to the valuable black opal. Black opal, opal that contains a black potch, is found occasionally in all mines, but it is most prevalent in Lightning Ridge and Mintabie.

Lightning Ridge black opal is found in two forms. It

Master Gemcutting Tips

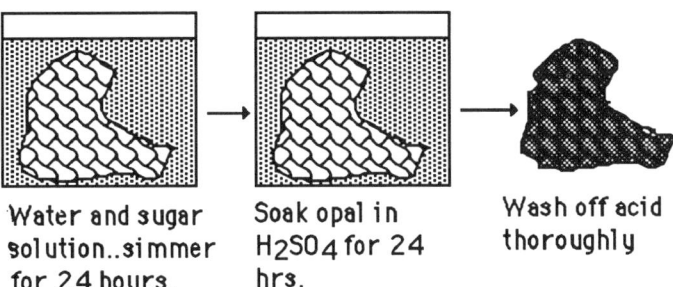

Water and sugar solution..simmer for 24 hours. Soak opal in H2SO4 for 24 hrs. Wash off acid thoroughly

Matrix opal from Andamooka is the type that can be treated to look like black opal. The formula calls for a 24-hour soak in concentrated suger solution and a dip in sulphuric acid which carbonizes the sugar.

is found with the color layer somewhere in the black potch and also in jell form with the black color functioning as an inherent element of the whole. Jell formed black opal is certainly far more valuable than the color layer-black potch type.

What makes Lighting Ridge black opal so distinctive is the fact that it's found in small nodules ("nobbies"). These appear as black or grey potch sections. When nipped on the edge or touched to a grindstone, the luscious opal color will often appear quickly.

Mintabie's opal is also founded mostly as black potch. Whether found as seam or "nobbies" it's best to cut them with a layer of the black potch on the back of the stone.

Not all that many American gemcutters are familiar with cutting boulder opal. This is unfortunate. Boulder opal is incredibly beautiful when a richly colored specimen is properly cut and polished. It is found for the most part in thin seams in ironstone. For this reason—plus the

Master Gemcutting Tips

expected difficulty of removing the color piece out of the host stone—boulder opal is cut and polished with a section of ironstone to serve as backing.

In the mining operations, some boulder opals split open through the middle of a color layer. Called "splits" these sections are seldom subjected to grinding or polishing because such activity would remove the color layer excessively.

When working with boulder opal, be prepared for a very messy operation. It's a dirty stone to work with and its brown-red sludge will get over everything. The character of the ironstone varies considerably from dense material (which can take a bit of polish) to porous (which is left

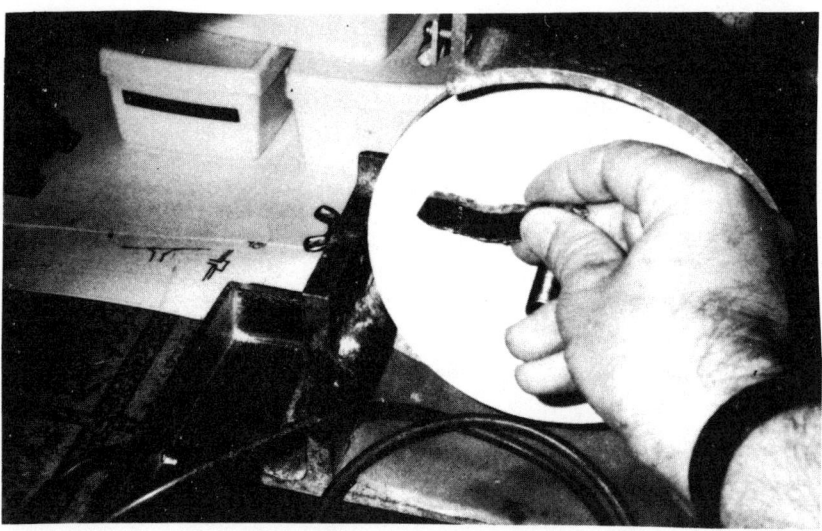

Polishing opal is straight forward. The formula in almost all cases calls for cerium oxide or tin oxide on leather. Some successfully use a felt wheel. If the opal is properly pre-polished at 600 or even 1200 grit, the polish can be expect to come up quickly and beautifully.

Master Gemcutting Tips

in its natural state).

Regardless of its density, the porosity feature suggests no oil when sawing or working. Plain water is best. If you can't avoid oil, rinse the sawed opal in a good detergent immediately after sawing in order to remove as much of the vestige of oil as you can manage.

More porous than boulder opal with colors that are not so prominent, matrix opal can be made into attractive cabochons. This material comes mostly from Andamooka and is worked like other opals with the idea of enhancing the opal particles to their best advantage. For some reason, matrix opal doesn't polish well with chemicals on leather. It responds best to diamond polish on a polypad.

Treating Matrix Opal....

Most gemcutters have heard of "treating" opal with sugar and acid to achieve the appearance of black opal. Andamooka matrix opal is the type used in this process.

When you've finished polishing a matrix opal it's color usually won't have the sharp color delineation or distinctness of other opal types. This is where treatment starts.

Make a strong sugar and water solution. That would be one cup of sugar to two cups of water. Heat the solution until the sugar has dissolved then put in the opal. Heat to a simmer just short of boiling, and allow this to simmer for 24 hours.

From time to time, you'll need to add water-sugar solution to replenish the liquid that has evaporated. If you can't maintain the simmer for a full 24 hours, turn off the heat, and resume with the simmering the next day. What you want is the full 24 hours of soak—without the liquid

Master Gemcutting Tips

turning to toffee—in the sugar solution.

Following the 24 hours soak, remove the opal, clean it in water only. Now place it in sulfuric acid for another 24 hours. The acid will carbonize the sugar particles and the stone will turn black with the colors shining brightly. Sugar-acid treated Andamooka matrix opal can be made to look just like good Lightning Ridge black opal.

Note: With all opal the best polishing technique is cerium or tin oxide on leather with moderate pressure. Some cutters use a hard felt polishing wheel with the oxides and get satisfactory results.

Again, the first sanding of opal should be done on a 360 or 400 silicon carbide wet paper then followed with a 600 grit. The pre-polishing step can usually be completed with a 1200 diamond unless you're working on a particularly good piece with firm jell. Then a 3000 pre-polish will finish off the sanding and effectively prepare the stone for final polish.

Depending on the material you can make an easy determination on whether or not you want to polish the slightly domed back. Some stones, such as a porous ironstone will make the decision for you, but once the final polish has been applied you have one of nature's finest offerings.

Troy vs. Avoirdupois . . .

How many carats in an ounce?
How many grams in a pounds?
What kind of weight is involved with a kilo?
Is there really a significant difference between the

Master Gemcutting Tips

troy and avoirdupois weight systems?

It's often not an easy solution for gemcutters who aren't quite certain what kind of weight they're dealing with. Just what a dealer has in mind when he specifies a price at so much per carat, gram or ounce can be an important consideration.

Many gemcutters get confused about weights. They have good reason for being in a quandary. Keeping in mind a few rules will help simplify the problem.

Most of the confusion arises from the fact that carats and grams are common to troy weight eg., TCG=Troy Carats and Grams. Ounces and pounds, though, are common to both avoirdupois and troy.

The lapidary field is one with a highly disciplined language, particularly with regard to weights and measures. All sizes of stones and gems have a specific nomenclature from "tiny particle" to "boulder".

Master Gemcutting Tips

Now comes the real mental crunch. The jewelry industry shifts around in its reference to the troy or avoirdupois scale depending on the amount of weight involves. There are 31.103 grams in a troy ounce vs. 28.35 in an avoirdupois ounce. A troy ounce also contains 155.5 carats vs. 141.74 carats to a avoirdupois ounce.

As a general rule, most weights over the carat or gram in the jewelry industry are common to the avoirdupois weight scale. Accordingly, these weights apply:

Troy (12 ounces=lb.)
1 pound — 12 ounces -- 5660 grains
1 ounce — 20 pennyweights -- 480 grains
1 ounce — 31.103 grams
1 ounce — 155.5 carats (metric)
1 gram — 5 carats
1 carat — .2 gram
1 carat — 3.086 grains

Avoirdupois (16 ounces=lb)
1 kilogram — 1000 grams, approximately 2.2 pounds (this is the "kilo" reference)
1 ounce — 141.5 carats
1 ounce — 28.3 grams
1 pound — 433.6 grams

Clark Standard Size for Rocks.
Particle — 1 mm or less
Fragment — 1mm to 1/8 inch

Master Gemcutting Tips

Pebble — 1/8 inch to 2-1/2 inches
Cobble — 2.5 inches to 10.5 inches
Boulder — over 10.5 inches

Do You Really Need Angle Splitters . . .

Many faceters work on older machines, ones which do not possess a mechanical angle splitter. Thus when faced with cutting instructions which call, say, for an angle of 42.7 degrees, these faceters find themselves in a quandary.

If your machine does not feature an angle splitter, must you give up on all those wonderful Meet Point instructions? Because Meet Point designs emerge from computer calculations the angles are often fractionally split. How can a faceter with no angle splitting function still

The one indispensable tool that every gemcutter should own is a reliable scale. Knowing the precise weights of rough and finished gemstones is vital for evaluating your work (yield?) and for pricing.

Master Gemcutting Tips

participate in Meet Point faceting?

The answer is really simple. Truth is, an angle splitter is not all that vital. You can easily estimate the fractional component of an angle and then bring in the meet points during pre-polish. How can this be done? The answer: by simple finger pressure.

Here is an example. Cut a facet. Let's say at 42 degrees. What we really want is a facet that is cut about 42.7 degrees. So, apply your finger pressure past the stop. You can count off seconds if you wish but a rough estimate is usually adequate. Most faceters have a pretty good idea how fast their machine or a particular lap will cut. Apply continued pressure about half the time it takes to cut a full degree. This could possibly be 3 seconds. If so, cut on for two seconds.

Lift the quill head so the facet is no longer cutting. The facet should now be completely clear of the lap and make no cutting noise. Stop the lap. Loosen the stop nut and lower the facet until it barely touches the lap again. What's the protractor reading now?

The protractor reading should indicate how much longer—if necessary—you must apply finger pressure "past the stop" to achieve a certain "overcut."

What about an error? What do you do if you overcut or undercut? Not to worry. Such a tiny error can be cleaned up later with a finer lap during pre-polish or polish. Besides, after practicing finger pressure for awhile you'll learn your machine's personality a bit better and your estimating will become quite accurate.

Cutting slightly past a stop and visually reviewing your work is what they mean by "...cut and look, cut and

Master Gemcutting Tips

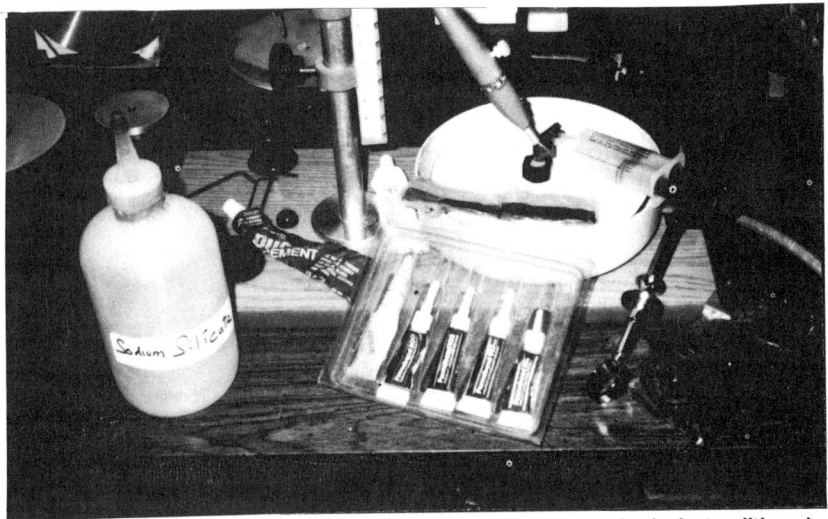

Many different materials are useful for dopping. These include traditional wax, superglues, fast acting epoxies, standard glues, two-faced tape, and even sodium silicate (water glass). Cornstarch is often added for stiffening purposes so the runny adhesives will remain in place.

look." Even with the verniers, you must still visually inspect your work to assure the meet points come in right.

Ridding a Buff of Contamination . . .

Contamination of a polishing buff or a polishing wheel poses a vexing challenge.

You'll know you've got such a problem when every stone starts showing small scratches e.g., cat whisker's no matter how careful you are. What's happened is that grit has penetrated the buff, or a crystal or dirt particle has imbedded itself in the wheel. One good way to check out a buff quickly is to keep on hand a series of cabochon shaped clear quartz blanks. When you are polishing and a scratch abruptly—and inappropriately— shows up

Master Gemcutting Tips

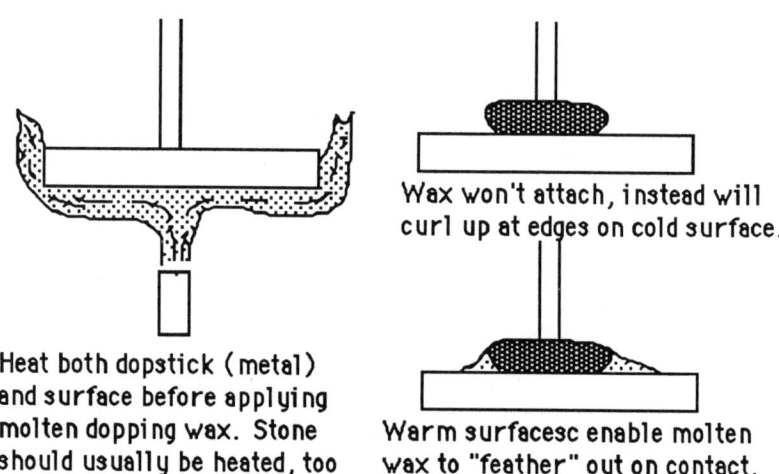

Heat both dopstick (metal) and surface before applying molten dopping wax. Stone should usually be heated, too

Wax won't attach, instead will curl up at edges on cold surface.

Warm surfacesc enable molten wax to "feather" out on contact.

When using wax as an adhesive, be certain that the mating surfaces of the mineral (wood doesn't need warming but a plastic or metal dopstick does) is warmed sufficiently. Otherwise, the hot wax will roll up, not adhere.

reach for one of the polished quartz blanks. Address it to the buff in question with some pressure for a few seconds. Then check the quartz cap with a magnifier. Did the quartz cap sustain a scratch, too? If so, you have a contamination problem—and a few more tests with the quartz cap in another area will confirm your worst suspicions. How to get rid of contamination short of throwing the buff or wheel away?

Get yourself a piece of balsa or even plywood. Hold the wood firmly against the buff while it's turning. The grit will usually penetrate the wood, leaving the buff clean.

On a lap wheel, the same treatment often works. Hold the wood firmly against the turning lap for a few seconds at a time. It will usually pick up the stray.

If these two methods don't work—and a check with the

Master Gemcutting Tips

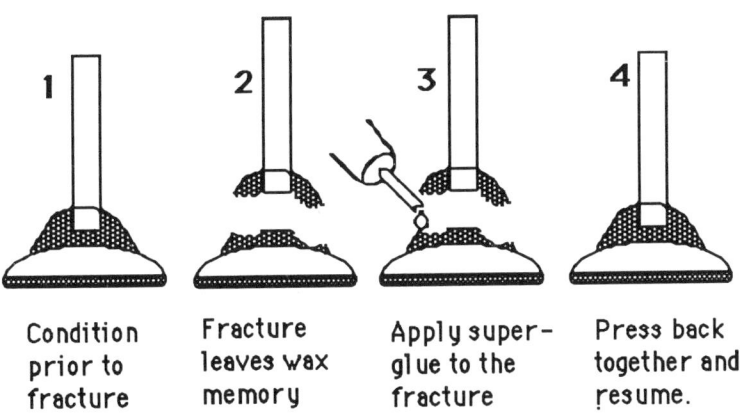

1	2	3	4
Condition prior to fracture	Fracture leaves wax memory	Apply super-glue to the fracture	Press back together and resume.

The principle advantage of dopping wax is that it leaves a "memory" whenever it fails or breaks apart. This is most helpful for re-attaching the mated parts and then continuing. The wax can be superglued or melted together.

---

same quartz cap will verify this—turn to a file or the unsharpened (but sharp corner) back of an ordinary table knife. Hold the file or knife blade back to the blade while the wheel is turning. This will almost always remove the contaminant (and some of the buff or wheel, too!).

Another approach to cleaning up a wheel is to hold the edge of a spoon against the wheel so the inside of the spoon faces the wheel. You can see the material coming off the wheel, including hard chunks.

Different Approaches in Dopping . . .

Regardless of the type of gemcutting you prefer, dopping is a critical operation.

Master Gemcutting Tips

Before most vital operations can be performed on a piece of mineral or crystal there must be some way to attach the stone to a stick, rod, or dowel. Mostly in this way does a gemcutter exercise the discipline over the stone so that cutting proceeds in a controlled sequence of operations.

For years, gemcutters relied on various formulations of dopping wax. Despite its shortcomings, dopping wax invariably performed well and predictably. That may explain why wax is still the favorite among many gemcutters, especially cabochon cutters.

Still, technology has offered some excellent alternatives in the last few years. It would behoove any gemcutter to investigate the benefits available with some of the new lapidary adhesives. In addition to waxes, gemcutters can now select from various cyanoacrylate (superglues), epoxies, urethane, special adhesives and glues, and even various tapes, including 2-face types.

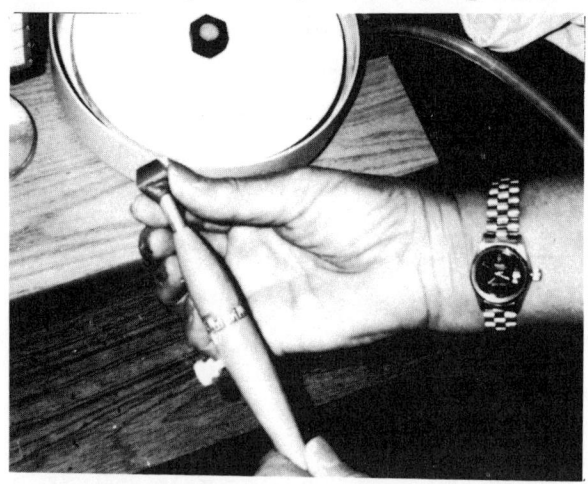

Wax Favorite...
Dopping waxes have many qualities, both good and bad. Yes, it's dirty to work with, creeps, and can inflict painful burns on the unwary. But that's about the extent

Master Gemcutting Tips

of valid complaints.

It's also inexpensive, can be reused within reason, is easy to form, and easy to remove. For all these advantages, the two great benefits of wax have always been its versatility and its ability to leave a memory.

The versatility factor comes from the many formulations and additives that manufacturers utilize. Waxes come in various hardnesses, different melting temperatures, and elasticity. Many of the waxes used, for example, for casting have remarkable elasticity and can be bent extensively before a fracture occurs.

A faceter, of course, wants none of this elasticity. He or she wants a hard, brittle wax— one that shows the least

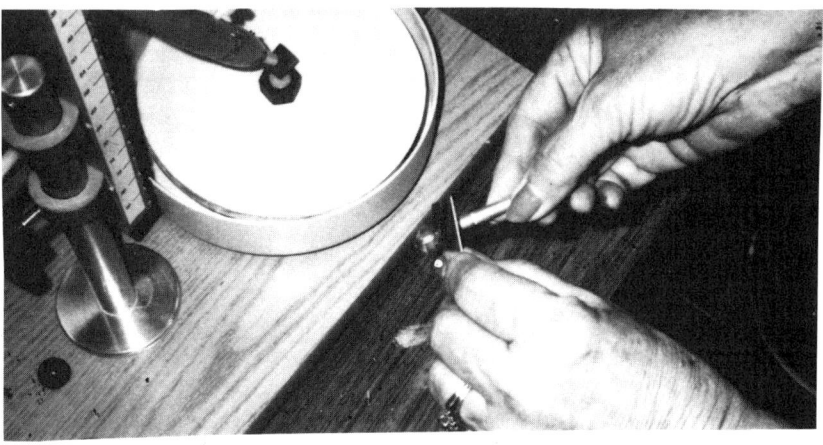

The benefits of superglues and epoxies is that they're not messy, work fast, and are easily removed. Superglue is tricky: it's bond breaks unexpectedly as well as in response to impact, water, and poor original matching. A sharp—hot— knife will usually cut through an epoxy bond.

Master Gemcutting Tips

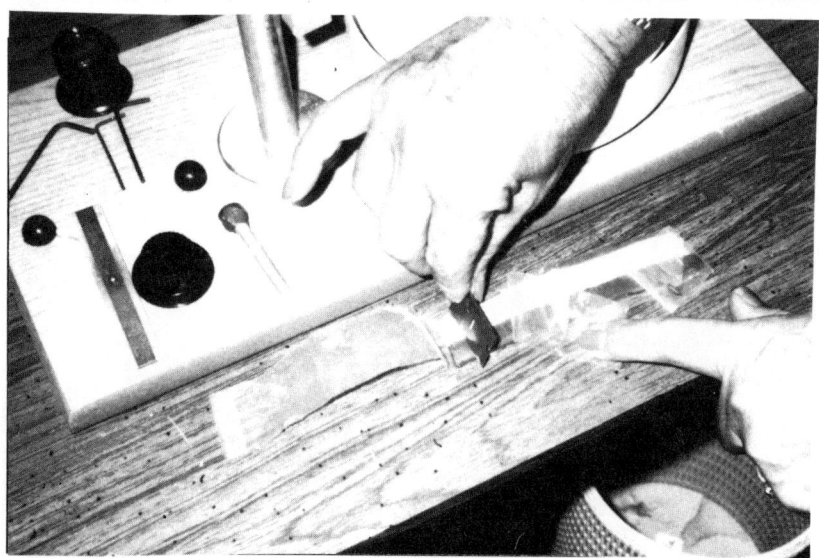

Duco's Ribbon Epoxy, available in most hardware stores, is the new epoxy of choice among many gemcutters because you can mix it cleanly in your fingers, enjoy plenty of working time, and remove the matured bond with a sharp Exacto knife blade. It's dynamite for transferring.

"cold creep." Cold creep is a term that describes the slight shift that wax will allow even when it's not molten. The creep is believed to come mostly from the warm fingers and other handling near heat sources which raise the temperature just enough that some shift takes place.

Because registration is so essential to a faceting operation, the faceter also wants a wax with a higher melting temperature. This guards against any tendency to cold creep and also allows the faceter to expose the stone-dopstick attachments to some heat without disastrous results eg., transfer dopping.

The handling of dopping wax is not complex. You can melt it by simply placing wax in a metal container

Master Gemcutting Tips

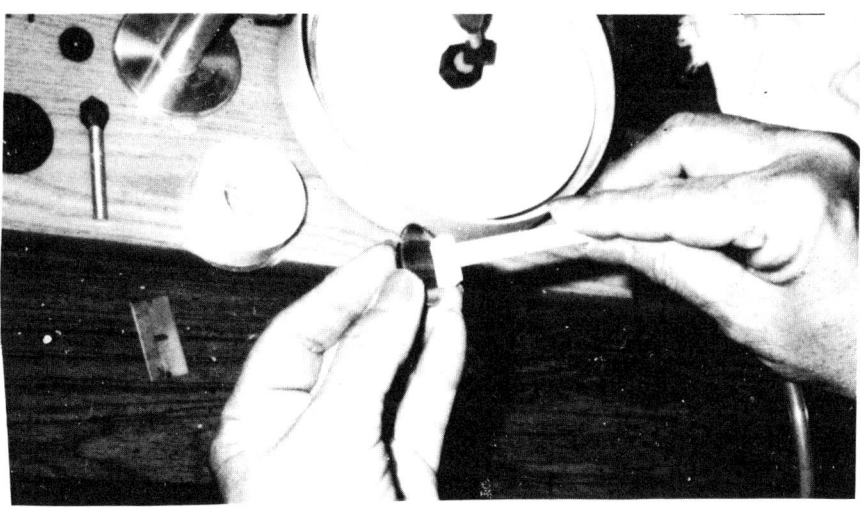

Many cabbers and carvers opt for two-sided carpet tape and the like for dopping cabs and flats. 3M tapes are also popular. Make sure you have surface area, though. Sodium silicate (water glass) is also handed by its a bit messy and difficult sometimes to control because of its runny nature.

---

over a candle light. Many gemcutters own small electric heaters specially made for melting wax. The candle and the electric heater serve a very useful purpose in that neither elevates the wax to temperatures that literally "burn" the wax, causing it to lose all its carefully developed holding qualities.

All wax manufacturers warn against overheating or exposing their waxes to direct flame. Many advise using their wax product only once. Most gemcutters, though, ignore this caution and go ahead with multiple uses with little penalty. Admittedly, most waxes do become more brittle with each re-use so using wax 3-4 times seems to be about the maximum usage.

Master Gemcutting Tips

Effective use of wax as a dopping agent involves no great technological feat. A user must simply keep in mind that wax solidifies as soon as it touche a surface that is cooler than the wax temperature. For this reason you must always use wood or pre-heated metal or plastic dopsticks. Wax simply won't "marry" with cold metal. Instead it will roll up every time upon contact before it has a chance to form a secure bond.

You don't have this problem with wood unless it has been chilled or wetted. Usually plastic will be sufficiently low in temperature that the wax will not immediately bond.

Wet Fingers...

Any gemcutter with wax experience knows that you should wet your fingers lest you expose yourself to a severe burn possibility.

When working with molten wax you need only to lick your fingers with your tongue or dip them into a convenient water supply. This is about all the protection needed, but without it the results can be painful.

Most cabbers heat a vat of wax until it is molten and then dip the end of a dopstick into the mass, gathering up a supply on the stick end. A quick finger twirl of the dopstick will form the wax so you can place a stone (pre-heated or shellac coated!) on the wax and then shape it with your fingers.

The stone is pre-heated for obvious reasons eg., so the stone will form a strong bond with the wax. With heat sensitive stones, it's best to paint some shellac on the surface that will meet the wax and allow it to dry. The alcohol content will soon evaporate leaving the stone's sur-

Master Gemcutting Tips

face coated with a hard layer of shellac. Once molten wax touches this dried shellac the latter will soften, "marry" the wax, and a firm bond will develop.

Technique differs when it comes to forming the wax. Some cabbers place the stone, top down on a table or platform, with the dopstick pointing straight up. With the stick-stone in this orientation, it is a simple matter to form the wax with your wet, cool fingers so it will secure the stone and dopstick in place. Other cabbers simply hold the stone-dopstick in their hands and work the wax into a shape that will provide a strong wax-stick platform for holding the stone.

To remove wax is simple. With a dopstick of any kind, you can place the dopped stone in an ice box or refrigerator. The cold temperature will cause the wax to shrink slightly and the stone will fall off.

A hot Exacto knife blade is the quickest and surest system of all. Just heat the blade and carve the hot wax away. What's nice about this approach is the total control you have over removal.

Superglue...
When gemcutters first started experimenting with the new miracle superglue, the popular name for cyanoacrylate, they hailed it as the answer to all dopping needs.

Then the bonds started breaking down a few too many times. Water and heat break down cyanoacrylate which resists pulling but not twisting and/or torsion or excessive vibration. Further, when the stone falls off the dopstick, it doesn't leave a memory as wax or epoxy does. And a CA bond fracture is often totally unpredictable.

Master Gemcutting Tips

The major drawback of superglue used to be its low viscosity. It just ran and ran and wouldn't fill up spaces created when an irregular shaped stone had to be dopped to a flat ended dopstick. If the stone had been tabled then the bonding was easier, of course. But superglue is poor for building up the sides, filling in open spaces, or increasing the dopstick's surface area in contact with the stone.

Faced with these shortcomings plus the prospect of starting over whenever the superglue failed, many gemcutters took the easy way out. They either went back to wax or to epoxy or some other type adhesive.

Superglue was saved, though, when manufacturers introduced accelerators. Accelerators are chemical compounds which support cyanoacrylates. They do just what their name implies: they accelerate the setting up of the bond. They do something else. They thicken the superglue and encourage it to fill in open spaces. With superglues today, you can indeed attach a rough stone surface to the flat end of a dopstick.

As for the loss of memory, many gemcutters now routinely superglue stones to a dopstick. If they need memory in case of a bond fracture, they put a ribbon of wax around the intersection where the stone and dopstick come together. Thus, should the superglue fracture enough fragments of wax will remain on the dopstick and the stone so that they can be fitted back together jigsaw puzzle style and cutting can be resumed.

How do you break down a firm CA bond? That's easy. You can heat the dopstick: heat destroys the bond. You can soak it in a strong solvent such as Attack or Acetone.

Master Gemcutting Tips

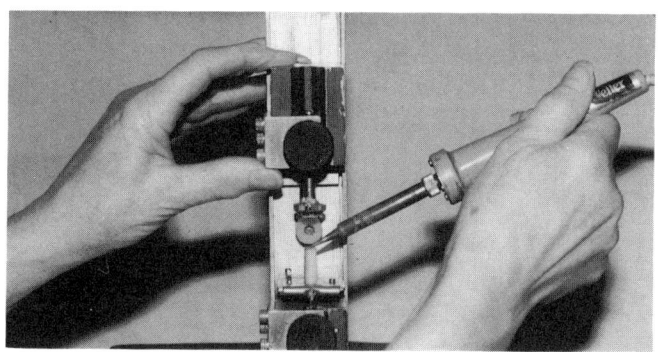

The Superior Dopping Method utilizes a special low temperature metal alloy as the dopping agent. This produces a "memory" match so that superglue can ultimately make a final, strong adhesive bond.

You can break it with impact. Hold the dopstick firmly in one hand and then rap it with another metal rod quickly and briskly. CA bonds come apart quickly because it doesn't like this kind of treatment. A less violent method involving the same principle is possible using a common tuning fork. Give the tuning fork a rap on something solid to get it vibrating and then merely touch one of the tongs to the dopstick. The CA bond will break apart instantly. Be advised, though, that sometimes a piece of your crystal comes off, too, when the CA bond is particularly strong.

Epoxies...

Once a gemcutter tries and is successful with a 5-Minute or other rapidly curing epoxy, chances are he or

Master Gemcutting Tips

she will remain with epoxy.

As a matter of fact, epoxies find most use in a hybrid dopping system. Many gemcutters, especially faceters, use wax on one portion of the operation and then use epoxy after the transfer. The reason for the double approach lies largely in the perceived difficulty of removing an epoxy bond.

Heating a dopstick will accelerate the polymerization so the epoxy will harden faster and stronger. The same heating will impair an epoxy's strength after it has hardened. Most gemcutters, though, cut or chip away the epoxy to remove a bond. An Exacto knife does a good job.

Because it takes considerably more heat to break down an epoxy bond, faceters often use dopping wax on the first half of a faceting project. When it comes time to transfer, they set up the second bond with epoxy, then apply heat to remove the initial wax bonding.

The heat melts down the wax quickly but only succeeds in making the epoxy bond stronger. With such an approach, the chances of the stone slipping out of registration is eliminated. With epoxy, the only heat involved is the exothermic reaction of the resin and the hardener. This represents no premature melting danger to the wax.

Ribbon Epoxy...

Lately, many faceters have opted completely for epoxy. Their brand of choice is the Duro Ribbon Epoxy, manufactured by the Locktite Corporation of Cleveland, OH.

This epoxy provides the best of all possible worlds to all gemcutters. The ribbon consists of two matching yellow and blue bands of chemical compound. When mixed together by hand they produce a powerful green adhesive.

Master Gemcutting Tips

It's clean. You merely cut off equal portions of yellow and blue ribbon and mix them in your fingers. No residue sticks to your hands. When the mixing is complete, the epoxy takes on a green coloration.

"This epoxy (Ribbon Epoxy) provides the best of all possible worlds to all gemcutters."

With no preparation other than clean surfaces of the stone and dopstick, the soft pliable epoxy—somewhat like a putty at this stage—is easily formed to hold the stone and dopstick together. The attachment is allowed to set overnight (that's the major drawback: it is not quick setting!) and then is ready for even harsh use. Not much material is needed to produce a powerful bond. Once applied properly in reasonable thickness, this epoxy bond simply won't break or fracture on you.

To remove the material is simple. Cut it off with an Exacto knife. It peals like hard wood and you can whittle through a thick portion in a short time.

Ribbon epoxy has other benefits. It stores for a long time without the need for special containers. It allows plenty of working time, something that most other adhesives don't. It can accommodate a heat buildup without cold creep or danger of breaking down. The only accessory needed is a sharp knife.

Other Adhesives...

Gemcutters are an innovative lot so many other adhesives are used for dopping.

Sodium silicate ("water glass") when mixed with corn starch makes a good dopping material. It's sensitivity to

Master Gemcutting Tips

A Meehanite cast iron lap offers valuable polishing assistance, particularly for stones with a MOHS 8 or higher. The porosity of the metal provides receptacles for diamond particles which prevents scratching.

water, though, makes it somewhat of a problem if the exposure length and intensity is greater than normal.

Normal glues from Wedgewood and Ross—when mixed with a thixotropic (non runny) agent—have been used with some success. The preparation and messiness of the material mitigates against any wide acceptance.

Special Alloy...

One new, unique dopping method has just been developed by Jack E. Moore of Redding, CA.

Jack calls his method—which utilizes a special metal alloy as the dopping agent—the Superior Dopping Method. The alloy is a cerro alloy, a low melting temperature alloy available with melting points of 158° F, 255° F, 281° F and 281° F to 338° F. It is furnished in ingots of 1 to 1.5 pounds.

Master Gemcutting Tips

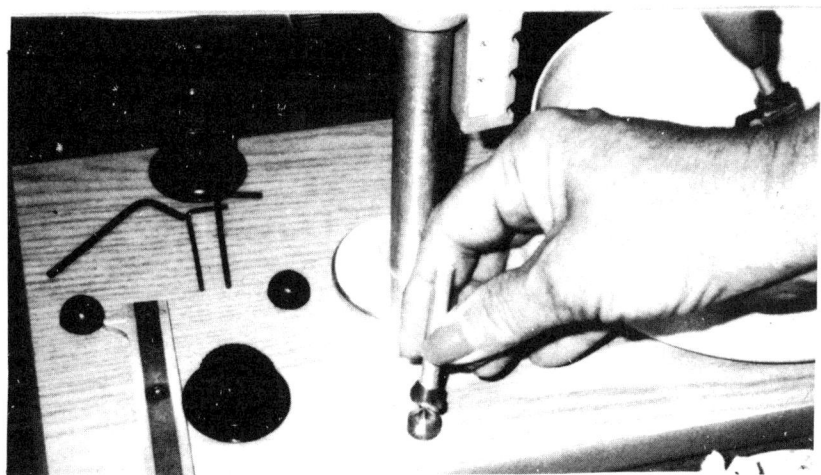

Don't overlook the beneift and the speed of an "open transfer" for faceting. All you need is a flat table, cut the pavilion first, and you can "eyeball" the crown dopping.

Low Temp Metal...

The Superior Dopping Method calls for recasting the alloy into 3/16" diameter by 3" long dowels. This makes the metal convenient for casting on the end of a dopstick.

Utilizing a flat surface on the gem so it will match closely the special "crown dopstick" with a cyanoacrylate as an adhesive, the Superior method comes into play once the pavilion and girdle have been faceted.

A special device called a "dopstick positioner" is attached in a sliding vee-block on the transfer jig to produce accurate alignment. Then a casting sleeve is fitted over the pavilion dopstick and the cavity filled with the special cerro alloy using a soldering iron to melt the alloy. This alloy head will eventually be used to grip the stone.

Master Gemcutting Tips

The pavilion dopstick is then removed from the casing sleeve by tapping on a rod which fits through a channel drilled lengthwise in the dopstick. A quick tap with a punch and hammer does the removal. The alloy containing dopstick is now prepared to accept the stone.

The cerro alloy is then simply sharpened in an ordinary pencil sharpener until its diameter is about 1mm smaller than the stone diameter. Masking tape, which holds the cerro alloy in place while it is being remelted, is next wrapped around the cerro alloy. The pavilion dopstick is fixed in the vee-block and the clamping screw is tightened so both dopsticks are held firmly.

The vee-block is slid until the stone touches the "pavilion dopstick" and an estimate of how deep you want the stone to penetrate the cerro alloy "head." The pavilion dopstick is then slid away, the alloy melted about 1/8" down with the soldering iron and then, in traditional dopping manner, the pavilion dopstick is shoved against the stone so it embeds in the liquid cerro alloy. The stone will not adhere to the cerro alloy: it will merely form a close fitting cavity.

Superglue is applied to the cavity and the stone is closed again into the cavity. A quick test of the bond is usually made before separating.

The crown dopstick also contains a center screw which is turned to release that end of the attachment. The transferred stone is now ready for cutting. Later when the stone must be removed from the pavilion dopstick, the cerro alloy is touched with the soldering iron and the stone is easily released.

The first two critical questions that a gemcutter will undoubtedly ask about the Superior Method is: one, can

Master Gemcutting Tips

this same procedure be performed using dopping wax as the adhesive, and two, what about dopping heat sensitive stones?

It probably could be used with wax although the stone would need to be warmed enough so that it would "melt" a cavity in the wax. You'd need a very low temperature wax. Low temperature waxes are notoriously low in strength.

As for heat sensitive stones, it would be a very unpredictable operation. Such stones can SLOWLY be brought to a relatively high heat without danger (it's quick change thermal shock that causes most damage with heat sensitive stones) prior to touching it against molten low temperature metal.

Master Gemcutting Tips

Index

A
abrasive action 69
abrasive numbering 70
abrasives 68
accelerators 152
Acetate 111, 115
Acetone 152
acid 25, 101
alcohol 24
alkaline 25
alloys 67
alumina oxide abrasive 70
aluminum pen 45
American Gemcutter
    Magazine 31, 61
American Society of
    Gemcutters 108
Andamooka 126
angle splitters 141
anode 10

antimony 67
apex facets 41
arbor nut 4, 113
Arizona, University of 108
asbestos fibers 35
Atlas Minerals 90
Attack 152
Australia 45
avoirdupois 138

B
baby shampoo 92
balsa 144
banker's rule 14
Barnett Gauge 50
basal cleavage 81
basic shapes 59
BC 70, 74
belt sander 133
beryl, polishing 65

Master Gemcutting Tips

bevel 48, 50, 54
black opal 134
blinking (stones) 105
blue print 113
boart 61
boron carbide 70, 72
boulder 141
boulder opal 135
brad 93
break facets 44
breaking superglue 44
bright lamps 53
brilliance 38
Bruce Bar 29, 62, 106, 115
Buehler Ltd. 31, 108
Bunsen burner 23

C

cab blank 46
cabochons, techniques 45
canvas buff 21, 30
carborundum 70
carvers 34
carving techniques 33
cast iron lap 1, 76, 80
cat hairs 101
cathode 10
CBN 70, 74
ceramic lap 1, 12, 24, 76,
ceramic master lap 77
ceramic polishing 12
cerium oxide 9, 29, 52, 65, 67, 70
channel laps 80
channel polisher 20
channels 58

charging 72
chromic oxide (abrasive) 70
chrysoberyl, polishing 81
Clark Standard 140
clay patties 22
cleavage plane 29
cloth polishing pads 108
cloudy film, opal 134
cobble 141
coffer dam 109
cold creep 147
colloidal silica 31, 91, 108
color 38
color enhancement 39
colored stones 37
common serpentine 19
concentric rows 85
cone of brilliance 38, 42
contamination 16, 143
Coober Pedy 126
copious flow (water) 30
Corian 67, 68
cornstarch 9, 57, 155
corundum, abrasive 70
corundum, polishing 65, 80, 81
critical angle 15, 37
cross hatching 48
Crystalite 31, 108
cubic boron nitride 70, 72
culet 39
culet 4
cutting break facets 4
cutting grooves 58
cutting large facets 64
cyanoacrylate 97, 151

Master Gemcutting Tips

CZ, polishing 65

D
damp-dry 101
DeBeers diamond designs 116
debris 79
deep scratches 16, 64
Delmar, Mfg. 10
depth sensor 5
designing carvings 58
diamond 72
diamond paste 75
directional hardness 72
dispersion 38, 41
dopping method 8, 18, 145
doublets, opal 74
doubly refractive stones 101
drilling 71, 93
Drunken Oval 119
Duco Ribbon Epoxy 148

E
electro-cleaner 10
electrolysis 10
emery 70
epoxy 56, 151, 153
even girdle 122
Exacto knife 151

F
Facetron 18
fancies 38
Fast Glue 89
feldspar group 27
felt buff 21
felt tipped pen 114
file, steel 144
fire layer, opal 131
fisheye 41
flash plate 10
flat cabochon back 54
fling 108
Formica 50
fracturing patterns 28
fragment 141
free wheeling 4

G
garnet 70
garnet, polishing 64
gate, splash pan 98
gauge examination 51
geometric channeling 58
girdle marker 49
glass, plate 53
grease pencil 115
grooves 58

H
Halogen floodlights 120
hand lapping 71
hardener 90
Hawke's Bay (NZ) 36
heat danger, stones 159
heat treating 22
heavy pressure 29
height, star sapphire 99
Hi-Dri 3
Horton, William 119

Master Gemcutting Tips

Hunt, Henry 27, 58
hydrogen concentration 26

I
illusion cutting 58
imperfections 99
insoluble ink 3
interesting cabochons 2
isoelectric point 27

K
Kerr's wax 103
kiln 23
Kleenex 11
Knoops 74
knurling tool 103

L
lamp wick 98
lap variety 63
lapidary abrasives 68
lapidary cement 112
large facets 32
Last Lap 22, 80
Lava soap 101
leather buff 21
LED 5
Lexan 67
light scratches 17
lighter fluid 104
lighting 120
Lightning Ridge 126
lighting, proper 120
Linde A 67, 105
Long, Bob 39

loose boart 69
loose diamond powder 75
loose grit 53, 71
low refractive gems 41
low temperature metal 157
lubricant 17
Lucite 21, 65, 67

M
Magi 114
magnesium 25
magnifier 55, 100, 129
making laps 66
man-made particles 71
maple lap 21
marking girdles 97
masking tape 91
matrix opal 137
matte Acetate 113
meet point designs 141
metal bonded laps 64
metallic oxides 69
Mintabie 126
Mirror Diamond Laps 107
Mirror Faceting Kit 110
mirror reflections 3
misalignment 109
MOHS 62, 68, 74
moonstone 84
Moyco 107
mud type sawing 71
Mylar 107

N
nails 8

Master Gemcutting Tips

Niahia Beach 36
non-cyanide 10
nonsoluble ink 4

O
oil 3
olive oil 65, 75, 107
onyx 9
opal 127
opal cutting 125, 128
opal, buying 127
open transfer 91
oxalic acid 9
oxidizer 101

P
Papier macé 123
parallel scratches 17
Paua shells 35
pavilion 4
pebble 141
pebble finish 102
peel-off adhesive 32
pelletized resin lap 22
Pellon cloth 32, 112
Pellon lap 21, 91
peridot, polishing 64
PH 25
phenolic disk 30, 64, 122
plywood 144
pock marks 100
polariscope 104
polishing abrasives 70
polishing corundum 64
potch 127

pre-polish methods 52, 63
precious (noble)
serpentine 19
preforming 64
production laps 76
profits 13
Prospector's Pouch 111
pyrometer 23

Q
quadrant wheel 82
quartz (flint) 70
quartz 9
quartz blanks 143
quick hardening epoxies 56
quick sawing setup 55
quill head 142

R
ray tracing 39, 41
razor blade 78
refractive index 37
refractory 74
registration, dopping 148
resin bonded laps 64
release form 95
removing CA 96
removing oil 3
repair dopstick 7
repair work 9
repairing stones 93
respiration mask 35
resurfacing laps 25
ribbon epoxy 154
river color 37

Master Gemcutting Tips

rocking motion 82
rough channels 60
rubber 8
rubber band 4
run the wheel 85
running stroke 86
running the wheel 82
rust 6

S

saving contents (can) 21
saw cuts (outlining) 34
scale, lapidary 141
scintillation 39
scratches 16, 53, 100
screwdriver 25, 46
sculptors 34
serpentine 18
serpentine divisions 19
shampoo 107
shape control 87
shapes 6
shards 73
sheet protectors 11
shellac 18
shellac coating 150
silicate particles (sand) 70
silicon carbide abrasive 70
silicon carbide wheel 59
silicone abrasive wheels 61
Sinkankas, John 113
sintering 72
slope 49, 83
slope cutting 85
slurry, polishing 17
Smith, J. R. 111

smoothing marks 16
sodium silicate 155
soft grain 72
solvent 44
special dopsticks 93
special metal alloy 156
Sperisen, Francis J. 67
spinel, polishing 81
spiraling 85
splits, opals 136
standard abrasives 70
starstone 84
steel washer 55
Steel, Norman 39
straight edge 53
Strickland, Robert 39
stripping pad 22
Sunflower Cut 115
sunstone 27
super abrasives 70, 72
superglue 151
Superior Dopping
   Method 153
swarf 79
synthetic diamond 73
synthetic spinel 68
syringes 75, 89
syringes 90

T

T square 50
table cut 91
tangent ratio 15
templates 45
thin polishing laps 105
thixotropicity 57

Master Gemcutting Tips

tick faceting 79
Tin lap 21
tin oxide (abrasive) 70
tin oxide 52, 65
tin/lead lap 105
titanium 23
toothbrush polisher 20
topaz, polishing 65
trace 47, 48
traditional abrasives 70
transfer 44
treating, opal 137
trim saw 46
triplets, opal 74
troy 138
tumbling 71
twinkle 39
two-faced tape 146
two-tone lap 115

U

Ultra Lap 77, 106, 107, 111
undercutting 47
Universal faceting
    angles 37

V

vee-block 157
Velour lap 21
Vernier 65
vertical sanding disk 54
vice, sawing 7
vinegar 67
vinyl 5
viscosity 108

W

walking the table 92
washout 39
water control 121
water glass 155
water on base lap 114
water splash 98
watery slurry 74
wax lap 102
wax, dopping 145
waxed string 122
WD-40 7
wet fingers 150
wetted tissue 97
wheat 22
White Cliffs 126
white light 38
wing nut 4
wiping motion 82
wooden dowels 8
Wykoff, Gerald 37

Y

Yogo Gulch sapphires 22